Grea
The

What Are

Great 3

Introduction: The Many Pleasures of the
    Smokies—and How to Enjoy Them 5

COVER: A fawn peers out from behind a tree on the nature trail in **Cades Cove** *(Walk No. 16). Deer are frequent sights in the cove.*

To John Leslie Winslow (1903-1992),
who would have loved the Smokies.

Great Walks

Text by Robert Gillmore
Photographs by Eileen Oktavec

No. 4 in a series of full-color, pocket-size guides to the best walks in the world published by Great Walks Inc. Guides already published: *Great Walks of Acadia National Park & Mount Desert*, *Great Walks of Southern Arizona* and *Great Walks of Big Bend National Park*. For more information on all Great Walks guides send $1 (refundable with your first order) to: Great Walks, PO Box 410, Goffstown, NH 03045.

Copyright © 1992 by Great Walks Inc.
Library of Congress Catalog Card Number: 92-70533
ISBN: 1-879741-04-0

What Are Great Walks?

Great Walks invariably offer beautiful and interesting world-class scenery and excellent views in the most picturésque places on earth.

Great Walks are also shorter and easier than the typical hike or climb. They're usually less than five miles long. They can always be walked in a day or less.* And they're almost always on smooth, firm, dry and, most important, *gently graded* trails. (Long, arduous, sweaty treks up rough, steep, rocky trails are a few things Great Walks are *not!*)

* One exception: a two-day excursion up Mount LeConte, where you spend the night in rustic, cozy LeConte Lodge.

What Are Great Walks Guides?

Great Walks guides carefully describe and, with beautiful full-color photographs, lavishly illustrate the world's Great Walks.

Unlike many walking guides, which describe *every* trail in a region, Great Walks guides describe only the *best* walks, the happy few that will delight you with their beauty.

Unlike many guides, which give you mainly directions, Great Walks guides carefully describe *all* the major features of every Great Walk so you can know, in advance, what the Walk has to offer and whether it's worth your time to take it.

After all, your leisure time is valuable. In your lifetime you can walk on only a fraction of the hundreds of thousands of miles of trails in the world. Why not walk only the best?

For your convenience Great Walks guides are an easy-to-use and easy-to-carry pocket size and our covers are film laminated for extra protection against wear and tear.

Acknowledgments

We are grateful for the assistance of Bill Hooks of Gatlinburg, Tennessee; Joyce McCarter of the Great Smoky Mountains Natural History Association; and Gene Cox, Glenn Cardwell, Donna Lane, Kitty Manscill and Bob Miller of the National Park Service.

Introduction: The Many Pleasures of the Smokies — and How to Enjoy Them

The Great Smokies should be treasured for many things: foaming white-water creeks… mesmerizing cascades and waterfalls… massive, dark green thickets of giant rhododendrons… forests of giant hemlocks that are moist even on dry days… layer after layer of the tallest mountains in the East extending infinitely to the horizon, each ridge a slightly paler blue than the one in front of it… the thick haze or "smoke" for which these hills are justly celebrated.

The Smokies' smoke and their spectacular creeks and cascades are the result of mountains and moisture. The Smokies are the largest mountain mass east of the Rockies. Sixteen of its peaks are more than 6,000 feet high. When you walk along the crest of the Smokies you are on one of the highest paths in the eastern United States — more than a mile above sea level. The Smokies are so broad and so high that they cause clouds to drop their moisture as they move across the mountains from west to east. The higher slopes of the Smokies get as much as 100 inches of rain every year, more than any other part of the United States except for the Pacific Northwest. The lower elevations usually get at least 50 inches a year and the rest of the mountains get something in between. That's enough water to make the Smokies a temperate rain forest and enough to inspire the famous epigram, "Rain, rain, Smoky Mountains is thy name." Much of this water is soaked up by the forest floor and helps the Smokies grow some of the biggest trees in the world. A lot of it, however, runs down the steep mountainsides to join the swollen creeks that rush down the narrow mountain valleys. So much water, flowing so steeply, in so small a space, over so many ledges and rocks creates some dazzling falls and rapids.

The Smokies' voluminous rainfall also helps cause its famous "smoke." This is how: Trees not only take in water through their roots; they also give off or "transpire" moisture through their leaves. The Great Smokies' forest is so large, and many of the trees in that forest are so big, that the total "transpiration" of moisture can actually form clouds. This tree moisture, along with the already moist air (and, sadly, some air pollution) is what produces the "smoke."

You can see this smoke, as well as the Smokies' most beautiful mountain, forest and water scenery, on 20 Great Walks, all of which are in or near the Great Smoky Mountains National Park.

The first 11 Walks take you, on well-graded trails, to major waterfalls. These Walks are arranged in order of length and difficulty, beginning with the quick .2-mile Walk to 100-foot-high Mingo Falls and ending with the 2.5-mile trail to 80-foot-high Rainbow Falls. Five of the waterfall Walks—Nos. 2, 3, 4, 5 and 8—follow wide, nearly level roadbeds. One Walk—No. 6—is paved. Seven Walks—Nos. 1-5, 8 and 10—feature not only major waterfalls but many minor ones as well, because they follow streams (known hereabouts as creeks, forks and prongs) for almost their entire length.

Walk No. 12 is a short, easy stroll through a parklike display of large trees, dense rhododendrons and cascading streams.

Walks No. 13-16 take you, on short, mostly level trails, to historic gristmills, farmhouses and other structures and exhibits that reveal the primitive life-styles of the Smokies' 19th-century pioneers.

Walks No. 17-20 offer exciting views of the Smokies' steep, sharply creased slopes. Walk No. 17 is a gentle, paved half-mile trail to the observation tower atop Look Rock, from which you can enjoy 360-degree vistas. Walk No. 18 offers not just one natural feature but four: parklike, creekside scenery, the natural tunnel of Arch Rock, the almost surreal Alum Cave Bluffs and 300-degree views of the many summits on both sides of the Newfound Gap Road. Walk No. 19 follows the Appalachian Trail for four miles along the crest of the Smokies to Charlies Bunion, site of what is arguably the most dramatic view in the national park. Walk No. 20 is a two-day excursion to the summit of Mount LeConte, where you spend the night at LeConte Lodge and enjoy often continuous panoramic views of many of the mountain landmarks in and around the park.

All the Smokies' Great Walks are accessible. Most begin at trailheads next to parking areas beside well-paved roads. A few Walks begin at the end of well-maintained and relatively short gravel roads. Every road, however, is scenic. Many follow a lively stream and the mountain views you'll see from your car will rival those you'll see on the Walks.

Three of the park's most popular highways are the Clingmans Dome Road, the Little River Road and the Newfound Gap Road. The second and third highways lead to several of the park's Great Walks. The first one, the seven-mile-long Clingmans Dome Road, is the highest road in the park and one of the highest in the eastern

United States. It follows the crest of the Smokies from the Newfound Gap Road to a parking loop just south of Clingmans Dome. The views of the North Carolina Smokies from here and from several overlooks along the way are worth the drive. So are the sunrises and sunsets from the parking loop.

The 17-mile-long Little River Road runs west from the Sugarlands Visitor Center, in the north-central part of the park. It passes several overlooks with views of Gatlinburg, Tennessee, then closely follows the twisting Little River into the Little River Gorge. The road curves between, and sometimes actually under, high, steep cliffs. You'll have almost constant views of the cascading rocky river and you'll pass two waterfalls: the Sinks, which is beside a bridge about two miles west of the Metcalf Bottoms Picnic Area, and Meigs Falls, which is about one mile west of the Sinks, on the south side of the road.

The 30-mile-long Newfound Gap Road is the only highway crossing the park. It links Gatlinburg and the nearby Sugarlands Visitor Center with Cherokee, North Carolina, and the Oconaluftee Visitor Center on the southern edge of the park. The road, or parts of it, is also one of the highest in the East. It climbs more than 3,000 feet to traverse the crest of the Smokies at Newfound Gap, which is 5,048 feet, or almost a mile high. More than half a dozen overlooks along the road provide some of the Smokies' best views.

Here is some more information as well as a few suggestions to help you get the most out of these Great Walks:

►Read the entire guide, or as much of it as you can, before taking any of the Walks. That way you'll be best able to select the Walks you want to take and you'll be familiar with the Walks before you take them.

►Carry the guide on all the Walks. (It'll fit easily in any pocket.) It gives you exact directions for each Walk, including how to get to the trailhead, as well as detailed descriptions of what you'll see.

►Follow our directions. The Walks start where they start, stop where they stop and go where they go for two reasons: (1) the trails we describe provide the best walking in the Smokies; (2) other routes or additional routes are more difficult, less scenic or both.

►You won't need a map to find or to take any of these Walks. All trailheads and trail junctions are well marked with incised wooden signs, every trail is easy to follow and we tell you everything you need to know to find your way. But if you like to follow a map anyway, or always like to know exactly where you are, or want help identifying some of the park's natural landmarks, get a copy of the park's official Trail Map. It's available at the Sugarlands Visitor Center, about two miles south of Gatlinburg on the Newfound Gap Road, and at the Oconaluftee Visitor Center, about a mile north of the Cherokee Indian Reservation on the Newfound Gap Road. The map indicates all roads in and around the park, as well as all major trails, creeks, mountains and other natural and manmade features. If you like to follow a topographic map, we recommend the waterproof edition of the Hiking Map & Guide to the national park, published by Earthwalk Press. It's sold at the visitor centers and other retail outlets.

►Tour the excellent exhibits of Smokies plant and animal life inside the Sugarlands Visitor Center. They'll help you identify the many species (especially of trees and shrubs) you'll see on the Walks.

►Unless you're in excellent condition (and few people are) do your body a favor: Take the easy Walks — Nos. 1-5 and especially Nos. 12-17 — first. They'll make it easier for you to take harder Walks — Nos. 6-10. Those, in turn, will get you in shape for the more taxing ones — Nos. 11 and 18-20.

►Since long-range views are clearest on sunny days, save the Walks with views (Nos. 6, 8, 11 and 16-20) for clear weather. Do the other walks on cloudy days.

►Any comfortable walking shoes are fine for the Walks that are paved (Nos. 6 and 17), that follow especially short and smooth paths (Nos. 2 and 12-16) or that follow smooth roadbeds (Nos. 2-5). For all the other Walks we recommend the greater support and protection provided by above-the-ankle hiking boots.

►Five Walks — Nos. 2-4, 7 and 8 — take place on trails that are used by horses as well as hikers. You usually won't encounter many animals but you might want to keep an eye out for an occasional dropping.

►If you don't like getting wet, we suggest you carry rain gear and wear waterproof hiking boots on cloudy days. For best protection, we recommend a hooded anorak and pants. The most comfortable rain garments are made of Goretex, which lets perspiration escape but keeps rain out too.

►Carry water on longer Walks. For best taste we suggest carrying it not in plastic or metal bottles but in ceramic canteens, such as the French-made Tournus. Here's a tip to keep it cold: The night before a walk pour a couple of inches of water in the canteen and put the canteen in the freezer. To make sure the canteen doesn't crack when the water freezes and expands, lay the canteen on its side and leave the top open. Next morning fill it up with cold water. The ice already inside the canteen will keep the water cold.

►It's wise not to drink water from any stream or spring in the Smokies (or anywhere else, for that matter) without boiling it or treating it with purifying tablets.

►Begin each Walk early enough so you can finish it comfortably before dark.

►Poison ivy grows beside some of the trails described in this guide. To make sure you avoid it, we suggest you stay on the trail.

►There are two poisonous snakes in the Smokies: rattlesnakes and copperheads. Both are extremely well camouflaged and very hard to spot in the normal forest environment—i.e., off the trail, which, happily, is where snakes almost always are. They're almost never seen on the trail and, when they are, they're much easier to spot than when they're in the woods. Conclusion: Stay on the trail. If you do leave the trail, especially near streams, inspect the ground ahead of you very carefully.

►Observe all safety signs in the park, especially those at waterfalls. To help conserve the park's natural resources, stay on the trails.

►Remember that the world's only constant is change. The locations of the mountains on these Walks won't vary from year to year. But some of the trees we describe may topple over at any time. And anything subject to human control—trail routes, parking lots, signs and so on—can change too. Be alert for trail reroutings, follow signs and consult the newest official maps and guides to make sure you have the most up-to-date information.

►We carefully describe the falls, cascades and other water features you'll see on these Walks. Keep in mind, however, that they may look different in unusually wet or dry weather.

When is the best time to take these Walks? That depends on what you like. And dislike. Walking is most comfortable in the fall, when the weather is cool and, for the Smokies, uncharacteristically dry. The leaves of the hardwood trees change color in October and the vistas from the ridgetops are best after late October, when the leaves have fallen and no longer block your view. On the other hand, the Smokies' beautiful herbaceous wildflowers (trilliums, phacelias, violets, lady's slippers, jack-in-the-pulpits, showy orchis, etc.) bloom in April, the tulip trees (also known as yellow poplars) and mountain laurel bloom in May, the orange flame azaleas and the pink catawba rhododendrons bloom in June and the white rosebay rhododendrons — the ones that grow along the creeks at lower elevations — bloom in July. Spring and summer, however, are very rainy in the Smokies and summer is also hot and relatively crowded. On the other hand, all that rain makes the creeks and waterfalls look their best. If you're lucky enough to be able to visit the Smokies more than once, the best thing to do might be to take the relatively harder upland Walks in the fall — you'll appreciate the cool weather — and do the shorter creekside Walks in July, when both the rhododendrons and the water will be at or near their peaks.

What are the very *best* Walks, the ones to take if you have time for only a few? We recommend Walk No. 1 (the best falls for the least time and effort), Walks No. 2 and 8 (for the most exciting cascades in the park), Walk No. 12 (a brief stroll through a natural park), Walk No. 18 (a kind of Smokies sampler, featuring a parklike creekside walk, remarkable natural features and an excellent view), Walk No. 19 (for what some consider the most exciting mountain vistas in the Smokies) and Walk No. 20 (a view-filled two-day trip up and down Mount LeConte).

Where should you stay? There are ten "developed" campgrounds, providing water and other facilities, in the park. The two closest to most of the Walks are Elkmont, which is off the Little River Road, about 6.5 miles west of the Sugarlands Visitor Center; and Smokemont, which is on the Newfound Gap Road, about three miles north of the Oconaluftee Visitor Center. There are scores of motels and other accommodations just outside the park in Gatlinburg, Townsend and Cosby, Tennessee, and in Cherokee and Bryson City, North Carolina. If you want to shorten driving time, pick accommodations that are closest to the Walks you want to take.

The easiest way to walk Mount LeConte is to make it a two-day trip (see Walk No. 20). The most comfortable way to do that is to stay at LeConte Lodge. The lodge, however, is booked as much as a year in advance. Nevertheless, if you don't have a reservation when you arrive in the Smokies you still may be able to get one because people sometimes have to cancel their trips. Just keep calling the lodge's reservation office at 615-429-5704 until it has a cancellation. Unfortunately, the lodge does not call people who are waiting for cancellations. *You* have to keep calling *them*. It may take several days of hit-or-miss calling but if you persist there's a good chance you'll get a reservation.

Getting to the Smokies is easy. If you're in a hurry you can fly into either Knoxville, Tennessee, or Asheville, North Carolina, and drive to the park, which is about an hour away from both cities. If you have lots of time and are coming from the Northeast, you can take the winding but beautiful Blue Ridge Parkway, which begins at the Shenandoah National Park in Virginia and ends just south of the Oconaluftee Visitor Center on the southern edge of the park. You can also take interstate highways, which come within 30 miles of park visitor centers.

1 Mingo Falls

This trip offers so much for so little. After taking one of the shortest, quickest walks in the Smokies, you come face to face with what is arguably the most stunning cascade in the region. Also, you can extend your walk by a mile and see the top of Mingo Falls, plus another, smaller falls, plus about 100 feet of exciting white-water creek.

Mingo Falls is on the Cherokee Indian Reservation, on the southern edge of the national park. The path to the falls begins about six miles from the Oconaluftee Visitor Center. You reach the trailhead via Big Cove Road, which begins on the Newfound Gap Road about a mile south of the visitor center and a couple of hundred feet north of the park-reservation boundary. The road immediately crosses the Oconaluftee River, turns left and quickly passes under the Blue Ridge Parkway. Then it follows Raven Fork, on your right, and passes several creekside campgrounds. Five miles from the Newfound Gap Road you'll come to a sign for Mingo Falls Campground and a bridge over Raven Fork. Here you'll also see a sign saying "Welch Campground" and, to the right of it, another sign saying "Fishermen Park Here." Leave your car by the second sign. Then cross the bridge and keep walking straight; you'll be on the wide, smooth, 300-yard-long trail to the falls. On your left you'll see a hand-painted sign on a tree saying "Mingo Falls" and a green-and-white-painted metal sign saying "Do not litter/Please take out what you bring in." You'll hear (but not yet see) Mingo Creek on your right. Also on your right will be a concrete cistern with a cyclone fence around the top of it. It's a holding tank for trout used to stock Raven Fork.

You'll barely start walking before you'll climb one of the steepest stretches of trail in the Smokies. This section, however, is only about 300 feet long, the equivalent of a few flights of stairs. And there are three log benches along the trail in case you want to rest.

The trail then levels off abruptly and you'll see Mingo Creek on your right. Then you'll pass a trail coming in on your left.

After walking past thick stands of rhododendrons and leucothoe on both sides of the path, you'll start to cross Mingo Creek on a wooden bridge. Here you look to your left, upstream, and suddenly there it is: Just 50 feet away and towering more than 100 feet above you is a natural water creation that's more than six times as tall as it is wide. Its dramatic verticality is stunning.

Mingo is not so much a falls as a tall but narrow ledge decorated with long, long ribbons of white water. The cascade begins as a six-foot-wide stream of white water falling over the top of the ledge. The stream quickly splits and, on the left side of the ledge as you face the falls, a single narrow stream of water cascades dozens of feet down to the rocky creek bed below. On the right side of the ledge, water falls in countless different ways: in tiny rivulets and cascades, in long, dainty ribbons, and in falls that look like tiny white stalactites clinging to the tops of caves. The creek creates even more, albeit much smaller falls as it tumbles over a jumble of rocks on its way to the bridge beneath your feet.

The trail ends at a log bench near the end of the bridge on the other side of the creek. If you turn around here and make the quick, easy return to your car, you will have walked only about a third of a mile.

If, on the other hand, you'd like to see the top of Mingo Falls, as well as another falls and some lovely white water — and if you're prepared to climb over some ledges and walk a slightly rougher trail to do it — follow these directions:

Start back to your car but, just before the trail begins its brief, steep descent, take the trail to the right, which is marked by a white-and-green-painted metal sign saying "TRAIL TO THE TOP." The path switches back and forth as it climbs up the steep slope. Go straight at the first trail junction you come to, go left at the next one — where the trail levels off — and go straight at the next three. On your way you'll have views of Raven Fork and the surrounding valley of Big Cove (valleys in the Southern Appalachians are often called "coves"). Less than half a mile from the beginning of the "trail to the top" the path follows about 30 feet of cyclone fence on your right. Immediately after the fence you'll cross a ledge on your hands and knees. The top of the falls is to the right of the ledge. A steel cable attached to the rock will help you make the very short but steep climb down the ledge to the creek. Be careful.

Long, delicate ribbons of water trickle down the ledge of 100-foot-high **Mingo Falls** *(Walk No. 1), one of the tallest cascades in the Smokies.* ▶

The top of the falls is a dramatic study in contrasts. Just above the falls the creek is narrow and flows through a dense grove of rhododendrons. Just a few feet downstream, however, the creek plunges into the open and spreads wide as it leaps over the ledge.

Go back to the path and keep following it upstream through a thick tunnel of rhododendrons. You'll have glimpses of small falls and cascades and hear them churning loudly in the creek to your right. In just about 50 yards you'll come to one of the loveliest natural compositions in the Smokies: In a shady grove of rhododendrons and leucothoe a 20-foot-wide, 20-foot-high sheet of water cascades over a green moss-covered ledge. The scene is a brilliant contrast of shimmering white water in the center of dark green moss, leucothoe and rhododendrons.

After you've enjoyed this special place, head back to your car and, if you like, take another look at Mingo Falls on your way.

2 Lynn Camp Prong Falls

Like the Walk to Mingo Falls (above), this easy round trip of less than a mile features fascinating views of falling water for very little effort. In fact, it brings you to what is probably the most exciting collection of waterfalls in the park. What's more, you can take the Tremont Logging History Auto Tour on your drive to the trailhead.

The Lynn Camp Prong Falls are in the northwest part

of the park. You reach the trail to the falls via the Laurel Creek Road. About .1 miles west of the "Townsend Y," which is where the Laurel Creek Road, the Little River Road and the road to Townsend, Tennessee, intersect about a mile south of the park boundary, turn off the Laurel Creek Road and onto a paved road marked with a sign saying "Tremont" and the "Great Smoky Mountains Institute."

In about two miles you'll pass the road to the institute on your left. Just after this intersection, on your right, you'll see a metal box in which you can pick up (for a nominal fee) a copy of the 12-page *Tremont Logging History Auto Tour.* The tour's seven numbered stops are along the remaining three miles of road (which soon becomes gravel) that take you to the trail to the falls. The pamphlet describes how, in this and other parts of the Smokies, lumber companies in the early 20th century built railroads, sawmills and entire company towns to harvest "one of the greatest virgin deciduous forests on earth." The numbered roadside markers indicate where railroads, skidders, pole roads and other logging infrastructure once stood. The pamphlet explains how this equipment helped extract the giant trees that were among the *billions* of board feet of timber cut in what is now the national park.

On the way to the trailhead you'll also enjoy views of the churning Middle Prong, which flows close to the road. Between the first and second stops of the auto tour, look for a 30-foot-high waterfall rushing into the creek on your left.

Shortly after the last auto tour marker, the road ends at a footbridge over Lynn Camp Prong. Leave your car in the parking area on the right. Then cross the bridge, from which you have a view, on your left, of lovely white water tumbling over the boulders in the creek bed.

On the other side of the bridge you'll see a wide, smooth gravel road following Lynn Camp Prong upstream. A wooden trail sign indicates that the road is the Middle Prong Trail. (Another trail, which the park has designated a "Quiet Walkway," goes off to the right and follows Thunderhead Prong for about an eighth of a mile.)

Like many creekside trails in the Smokies, the Middle Prong Trail was once the bed of a railroad built to haul newly harvested timber. That's why the trail, and others like it, are among the widest, smoothest, most gently graded walkways not just in the park but in the entire world.

The Middle Prong Trail rises gradually above Lynn Camp Prong as it follows the creek upstream. Rhododendrons, leucothoe, hemlocks and various hardwood trees flourish on both sides of the path. But the woods between the trail and the creek are open, so you have excellent views of the cascading stream below you. In fact, the trail is a perfect linear observation platform from which, as you walk, you can watch one- to three-foot-high cascades fall over rocks in the stream.

You'll stroll less than a third of a mile before you come to a log bench on your left and the first of more than half a dozen notable waterfalls you'll see in the next 1,000 feet. This falls is the largest one of all. It's the result of a sloping, 20-foot-high ledge that forms a natural dam across the creek. The stream rushes over the lowest part of the top of the "dam," then flows down the ledge in a long S-curve,

These falls on **Lynn Camp Prong** *(Walk No. 2) are one of the most stunning natural water compositions in the Great Smokies.* ➤

spreading elegantly across the rock as it falls toward a large pool below. Rhododendrons on both sides of the creek form a dark green, leafy frame for the gray ledge and the white water falling over it. Downstream the creek is a series of terracelike pools bordered by rocks and more rhododendrons.

The trail then curves to the left to follow the twisting creek — and the falls — upstream. In just a couple of hundred feet you'll come to another bench on your left. From here you can look down at the top of the falls and a thrilling display of water surging over ledges. Upstream, on your right, water gushes in a foamy sheet over a 20-foot-high, 30-foot-wide ledge that spans the width of the creek. Just below that ledge another, six-foot-high one also spans the creek. Water flows over it in thin, transparent, fan-shaped sheets that fall into a deep triangular pool in the ledge. Then the water slides transparently over another ledge into a 40-foot-long spillway formed on its upstream side by the ledge and on its downstream side by the top of the "dam" that creates the first falls. A foaming three-foot-wide stream of white water surges down this spillway before leaping over the rock dam.

The dry portion of these large ledges is a convenient platform on which to sunbathe, picnic and enjoy this dazzling water show close up. Also look for the graceful three-foot-long, two-foot-wide pothole that has been ground in the ledge by centuries of water-borne rocks.

Together these cascades form more than 150 linear feet of some of the most fascinating white water in the Smokies. But they're only the beginning. Another falls is just ahead. You can't see it from the trail but here's how to find it: Go back to the trail and walk about 100 feet ahead. Then walk between the large rocks and rhododendrons on the left of the trail. Ahead of you will be a moist, shady glen where two eight-foot-high falls bounce off a ledge, leap up like the water in a gigantic drinking fountain, then drop into a lovely, six-foot-wide, 40-foot-long pool rimmed by smooth mossy ledges that slope gently into the still water.

Return to the trail, walk just a few hundred feet more and you'll come to one of the most stunning natural water compositions in the park. It's not one falls but many and it must be seen not from the bench opposite the falls farthest upstream but from the bottom of the falls farthest *downstream*. Viewed from there, on the edge of the creek, a few feet to the left of the trail, Lynn Camp Prong is not so much a stream as it is a rough, natural version of an elaborate, 30-foot-wide, 100-foot-long Italian Renaissance villa garden, built around water falling down a hillside in Tuscany. Upstream are three falls, each one wider than it is high. The one farthest away is about two feet high and eight feet wide. The one just below it is about five feet high and six feet wide and the one furthest downstream is about one foot high and eight feet wide. Below the third falls are two smaller ones that drop into a terracelike pool. Out of this pool, through notches in its ledge wall, flow three different falls, each one about six feet high and between two and four feet wide. All three falls flow into a deep pool in the ledge that's foaming with white water, like a huge natural jacuzzi. You can imagine water nymphs, or even more mundane creatures, frolicking here. The stream then spills over the edge of the pool in a six-foot-wide, three-foot-high fall that crashes, frothing white, against more ledge on the bank of the stream. Small *jets d'eau* darting through the moss at the edge of the "jacuzzi" appear to be coming through the ledge itself. The jets turn on and off like the so-called water tricks of Italian Renaissance gardens. And, like many Italian villa gardens, this lovely balanced water composition ends in a large pool, 20 feet wide and 40 feet long.

Return to the trail and walk upstream 100 feet or so to the bench on the left for another view of this natural water garden. You can see how the garden's pools and falls are created by parallel green, moss-covered ledges that span the width of the creek like dams.

You've now seen the most remarkable falling water on Lynn Camp Prong. If you turn around here and head back to your car you can enjoy all the falls again and you will have walked less than a mile. If, on the other hand, you'd like to extend your walk you can keep following the creek upstream. The trail remains gentle and the creek stays lively (if less spectacular) for at least another mile.

3 Twentymile Creek Cascades

Like the Walk to the Lynn Camp Prong Falls, the trip to the Twentymile Creek Cascades is a relatively short (.6-mile), nearly level Walk to a beautiful series of cascades and one of the most exciting streams in

Twin falls on the 100-foot-long **Twentymile Creek Cascades** *(Walk No. 3).*
▶

the park.

The cascades are in the southwestern edge of the park, about six miles from Fontana Village, North Carolina. You can get there from two directions and both routes are interesting.

If you're driving to the trailhead from Cherokee, take Route 19 west to Bryson City, then Route 74 to Route 28, which will take you to the trailhead. Just east of Fontana Village on Route 28 you'll have a view of Lake Fontana on your right. The long lake, which lies along the southern boundary of the park, was created by Fontana Dam, which was built during World War II for hydroelectric power. The 480-foot-high dam — the highest east of the Rocky Mountains — is about a mile from Route 28. Pamphlets and exhibits at the visitor center explain the history and operation of this and other Tennessee Valley Authority dams in the area. Fontana Dam is about two miles from Fontana Village, which was constructed to house some of the thousands of people who built the dam. The village is now a resort and its restaurants, marina and other facilities are open to the public. From the village to the trailhead, Route 28 mostly follows the Little Tennessee River, which drains Lake Fontana and flows into Lake Cheoah, which also was created by a TVA dam.

If you're driving to the trailhead from Tennessee, the shortest route is to go to Cades Cove via the Laurel Creek Road. Just after the Cades Cove Visitor Center take a right onto the Forge Creek Road, which is gravel. In about two miles turn right onto Parson Branch Road, an unpaved, narrow, one-way, eight-mile-long track (that, incidentally, is not open in the winter). The road climbs through the forest to the crest of the Smokies. Then it follows its namesake, Parson Branch, crisscrossing it on cement fords several times before joining Route 129 on the southern boundary of the park. Go left at this intersection. In 4.7 miles you'll be at the junction of routes 129 and 28. Turn left onto Route 28, which follows Lake Cheoah all the way to Twentymile Creek. In 1.5 miles you'll see a small waterfall on your left. In another 1.5 miles the road runs downhill to the head of a pretty cove where Twentymile Creek flows into the lake. A sign on the left, just before the bridge over the creek, says "Twentymile Ranger Station." Take a left here, drive past the ranger station, on your right, and leave your car in an unpaved parking area, also on the right, about .3 miles from Route 28.

Another 100 feet up the road, just past a vehicle gate, is a wooden sign marking the beginning of the Twentymile Trail. The trail is a continuation of the road you rode in on. It's wide, smooth, gently graded and gently curved. Rhododendrons, leucothoe, hemlocks and hardwoods grow on both sides of it and Twentymile Creek rushes past on the right.

You'll quickly pass the stable and corral of the ranger's horse, also on your right. In less than half a mile you'll cross the boulder-choked creek on a wooden bridge. On the other side of the bridge the Wolf Ridge Trail goes left and the Twentymile Trail goes right. Take a right. After less than 200 feet of gentle climbing you'll see a sign on your right saying "Twentymile Creek Cascades."

The 150-foot-long trail from the sign to the cascades leads you to more than water: It takes you to one of the loveliest scenes in the Smokies. Here, in the middle of a small, moist glen, snow-white water creates a brilliant contrast to the dark green foliage of moss, hemlock, rhododendron, leucothoe and laurel.

The 100-foot-long cascades begin upstream with twin six-foot-high falls surging down a green mossy ledge. The cascade on the left is two feet wide at the top but fans out to six feet wide at the bottom. The cascade on the right is eight feet wide from top to bottom. Both pour into a frothing three-foot-long, 20-foot-wide pool. From this pool another fall, two feet high and two feet wide, drops into a 20-by-20-foot pool. The creek makes still more cascades as it moves over the ledges that span the width of the stream like steps. Sometimes the water falls in a white gush. Sometimes it slides transparently over the gray ledge. Sometimes it surges through narrow rock channels. The dozens of little water sideshows are fascinating. Finally, at the bottom of the cascades, the stream falls into a 10-foot-long, 40-foot-wide pool surrounded by hemlocks and rhododendrons.

In the English Lake District a waterfall is called a "force." The name fits the cascades. Other falls in the Smokies flow more leisurely. These small but powerful rapids pummel every rock in their way.

If you like you can turn around here and retrace your steps to your car. On the other hand, the creek is one of the liveliest streams in the park and the trail you're on is one of the gentlest. So if you're in the mood for more easy walking and more trailside views of white water, keep going.

If you go another mile, you'll come to another bridge and, shortly after that, to a third bridge. Upstream from

Twenty-five-foot-high **Indian Creek Falls** *(Walk No. 4) are covered with autumn leaves.* ▶

the last bridge the creek is a lovely 20-foot-wide, 30-foot-long pool surrounded by rhododendrons. It's a fit climax to a Great Walk.

4 Indian Creek Falls & Toms Branch Falls

This easy two-mile round trip features not one but two major falls—one of which is only 1,000 feet from the trailhead—and continuous views of a cascading creek.

The Walk is near the southern edge of the national park, just north of Bryson City, North Carolina. To get to the trailhead take Route 19 to the center of Bryson City (about ten miles from Cherokee). Turn north onto Everett Street. Go .2 miles and take a right onto Depot Street. After .1 miles take a left onto Ramseur Street and in just 50 feet take a right onto Deep Creek Road. (All these turns are marked by brown-and-white park signs saying "Deep Creek Campground.") Follow Deep Creek Road 2.2 miles to the park entrance. Enter the park and drive past the campground and picnic area. Deep Creek (which is wide but actually not much deeper than other park creeks) will be on your right. About .4 miles after the park entrance the road becomes gravel and, shortly after, ends in a parking area by the creek.

The trail officially begins at a gate across a road beside the parking area. A sign there marks the Indian Creek Trail and tells you that Indian Creek Falls is one mile away and that Toms Branch Falls is only 1,000 feet ahead. You can also begin your Walk, however, by following a path that begins at the northern end of the parking area. This trail follows the creek through the woods and, just 150 feet after it starts, joins the Indian Creek Trail. We recommend the 150-foot trail.

In any event, the Indian Creek Trail is easy. It's another wide, smooth, mostly level roadbed that rises and curves gently and stays very close to the creek on your right. You barely start experiencing the trail, however, when you reach Toms Branch Falls.

Like the Huskey Branch Cascades (Walk No. 5) and Mouse Creek Falls (Walk No. 8), Toms Branch Falls occur when one stream (in this case Toms Branch) flows over a steep ledge into another stream. The result is a more complex and therefore even more interesting water feature than the falls alone. Instead of an essentially one-dimensional feature — the falls moving down their vertical axis — there is a two-dimensional one: the falls flowing on their vertical axis and the larger creek flowing on its horizontal axis, together creating moving water that's much more dynamic than merely the sum of its two parts.

You can watch Toms Branch Falls, which are on the other side of 30-foot-wide Deep Creek, from a 10-foot-long log bench just to the right of the trail. (Be sure not to touch the poison ivy growing on the huge moss-covered oak in front of you.) The site is not as much a series of "falls" as it is a mossy gray ledge elaborately decorated with many kinds of falling water. The 50-foot-high falls begin at the top of the ledge in a narrow, six-foot-long trickle of water. Then the water proceeds to the bottom of the ledge, first in three 15-foot-high trickles, one beside the other; then in two white, 16-foot-long streams of water sliding

transparently over the ledge; then in half a dozen streamlets, sometimes gliding transparently over the ledge, sometimes falling in two- to six-foot-high white drops, eventually splashing onto a ledge near Deep Creek and finally running into the creek over a long ledge on the bank.

Soon after Toms Branch Falls the trail crosses the creek on a large wooden bridge. Just upstream a foot-high ledge creates a natural dam over which flows a low, 20-foot-long waterfall that's as wide as the creek. A 12-foot-long log bench beside the creek here offers you a chance to sit and enjoy the view.

Then the trail climbs gently until it rises 50 feet above the stream. The path is now a linear observation platform—like the Middle Prong Trail—and it gives you a bird's-eye view of rapids, small cascades and other white water in Deep Creek.

About .7 miles from the trailhead the trail splits. The Indian Creek Trail goes to the right, following Indian Creek, and reaches Indian Creek Falls in just 200 feet. The Deep Creek Trail crosses the bridge over Indian Creek in front of you. Before you go to Indian Falls, walk down to the bridge and look upstream. The creek, surrounded by large rhododendrons and leucothoe, surges through a tiny gap in the mossy ledge, which turns Indian Creek into a narrow frothing white falls.

Now return to the Indian Creek Trail and walk to Indian Creek Falls. A wooden sign by a log bench on the

Cascades in the Little River, one of the liveliest streams in the Smokies, seen on the trail to the **Huskey Branch Cascades** *(Walk No. 5)*.
◄

left of the trail marks the beginning of a 60-foot-long side trail down to the base of the cascades.

Indian Creek Falls are as simple as Toms Branch Falls are complex and as bold as the latter are delicate. A 30-foot-wide, 25-foot-high ledge creates what looks like a dam across the creek and two thick streams of water gush side by side down the 45-degree slope of the ledge. The stream on your left is between four and six feet wide and falls straight down to the 25-foot-long pool that spans the entire 30-foot width of the creek. The stream on your right, which is partly obscured by rhododendrons, is four feet wide when it starts falling. But before it reaches the pool it's split by rocks in the ledge, gently curves to the left and widens to ten feet — four feet wider than the stream to the left. If you look carefully you can sometimes see a third cascade — a faint, foot-wide wisp of water trickling down the left-hand side of the ledge.

Go back to the trail and follow it to a bridge about 200 feet farther upstream. On route you can see Indian Creek tumble over ledges and rocks, creating some of the most luscious white water in the park. It's a nice ending to your Walk before you turn around and head back to your car.

5 Huskey Branch Cascades

The 35-foot-high upper cascades of **Laurel Falls** *(Walk No. 6).* ▶

This nearly level, two-mile round trip takes you along one of the Smokies' largest, liveliest creeks to one of the most charming cascades in the park.

The Walk is in Elkmont, in the north-central part of the park. To get there take the Little River Road to the road to Elkmont Campground. This intersection is about five miles west of the Newfound Gap Road and about 13 miles east of the Townsend "Y," in the northwest part of the park. From this junction follow the road 1.5 miles to the entrance of the campground. Go left here on another road marked with a wooden trail sign that tells you (among other things) that the Little River Trail is 1.5 miles ahead. After passing the campground on your right you'll come, in .6 miles, to a fork. Go left again. The road soon becomes gravel, then follows the Little River for about .7 miles until it comes to a parking area on the left. The trail begins a few feet ahead at a vehicle gate.

The path is a former railroad bed. It's wide, smooth and nearly level. Sometimes it curves close to the Little River, letting you see its dashing white water for much of your walk. And even when you can't see the water you can usually hear it. Occasionally the trail straightens out and becomes a long *allée* of maples, poplars and other hardwoods.

The last time we were there was on a morning of dazzling contrasts. The sky was blue and sunlight pierced through the rhododendrons and trees ahead of us. It had rained hard the night before so the air was clear. Shafts of sunlight contrasted with deep shadow. Sunlight also glistened on the water that remained on the leaves so the woods sparkled with nearly blinding specks of pure white light. The white light was a stunning contrast with the dark green leaves and the dark tree trunks. The light made the darkness seem darker and the greens greener. The shadows and the trees, in turn, made the white light nearly incandescent.

Just a few hundred feet from the trailhead you pass a long bench on your left.

In about half a mile you pass another bench, also on the left. Here a cluster of rocks in the river creates a thick knot of little falls.

Then the trail goes briefly away from the stream and, just over a mile from the trailhead, comes back to the river and crosses Huskey Branch on a wide wooden bridge. Above, below and beneath the bridge are the Huskey Branch Cascades. Like Toms Branch Falls (Walk No. 4) and Mouse Creek Falls (Walk No. 8), the cascades occur as the stream on which they're located empties into another creek.

Like Toms Branch Falls, this site is more than falling water. It's actually a 100-foot-long rhododendron garden whose linear focal point is a mossy green ledge with a beautiful white-water stream running down the middle of it. From the bridge you can look upstream at a one- to two-foot-wide, 25-foot-long ribbon of white water flowing down a curving trough in the ledge. Above this cascade is another six-foot-high falls. Huge rosebay rhododendrons, their stems as thick as the trunks of small trees, crowd both sides of the creek. Their dark green, six- to eight-inch-long leaves reach out over the falling water.

Climb carefully up through the moist thicket of rhododendrons to the left of Huskey Branch and you can see how the creek cascades into a series of pools. The scene is powerful in its simplicity. The pools are uncluttered depressions in the ledge. The major plants are all one species: ancient rosebay rhododendrons. In the perpetual shade, the white water is a startling accent amid the dark green of their leaves and of the moss that grows on the ledge.

When you're ready, turn around, retrace your steps to your car and enjoy the Little River from another perspective as you follow it downstream.

6 Laurel Falls

This easy but dramatic 2.5-mile round trip offers many things for relatively little effort: a self-guided nature trail, views across the Little River Valley to Meigs and Blanket mountains, and one of the largest falls in the park. In fact, this Walk is so popular that the Park Service paved the trail to keep it from wearing out.

The Walk begins on the north side of a parking area on the Little River Road, 3.6 miles west of the Sugarlands Visitor Center. Before you start pick up the handsome *Laurel Falls Self-guiding Nature Trail* pamphlet in the box at the trailhead. It's a good introduction to the Smokies' major trees, shrubs and forest types.

The asphalt path winds gently up the relatively dry,

Grotto Falls *(Walk No. 7) is a 20-foot-high curtain of water in front of a 20-foot-deep grotto after which the falls is named.* ▶

steep southern slope of Cove Mountain. The land rises sharply on your right and falls steeply on your left. The woods here, mainly oak and pine, are very open — you can see hundreds of feet into the forest. You'll pass lots of mountain laurel, which (as the nature trail pamphlet explains) does well on dry soil. On the other hand, you'll see rhododendrons, which need moisture, mainly near the tiny creeks that flow down the narrow creases in the side of the mountain.

At nature trail marker number 6 you'll start hearing the falls. At marker number 7 you'll be at what the brochure calls a "picture window." This is a classic Smoky Mountain view. You look down through the steep-sided valley of Laurel Branch (which creates the falls you'll come to shortly) and across the Little River Valley to Meigs and Blanket mountains. The mountains are a series of blue ridges, each one slightly lighter than the one in front of it.

As the trail gets closer to the falls, the Walk gets more dramatic. The sound of the falls gets louder and the slopes on both sides of the trail get steeper and steeper. Just before the falls, the lichen-coated rock outcrops on the right of the trail rise as much as 20 feet and the bank to the left is almost a sheer drop to Laurel Branch, 50 feet below. If you're afraid of heights, don't worry: The trail is wide and the bank is covered with trees and shrubs, so you won't feel uneasy. Make sure, however, that you don't step in the poison ivy on the left side of the walkway.

The paved trail ends at the flat, 20-foot-long, 40-foot-wide ledge that separates the upper and lower cascades of Laurel Falls. You're now literally in the middle of the falls. Cross the creek, which flows over the ledge, on the large rocks scattered across the almost-level sandstone, sit down on the log bench or on the ledge itself and enjoy the water view.

The falls occur because Laurel Branch must negotiate a 75-foot-high rock outcrop on its way to the Little River. At the very top of the 35-foot-high ledge upstream, the creek splits and two streams of water splatter down to a basin in the rock. Then the creek divides again and three cascades flow into a shallow 30-foot-wide pool formed by the ledge you're standing on. The entire upper falls is framed by rosebay rhododendrons.

The lower cascades are even higher than the upper ones. They begin when the creek slides off the ledge you're standing on. Then they fall over the right side of three massive horizontal rock outcrops to drop a total of nearly 50 feet to a pool below.

If you'd like a view of both the upper and lower falls at once, cross the creek, walk about 100 feet and turn around. You're not as close to the falls here as you were and your view, unfortunately, is partly obscured by trees. But you can still see the whole show, from the top of the upper falls to the bottom of the lower ones, and even some white water downstream. In fact, on no other Walk in the park can you see so much falling water all at once for so little effort.

When you're ready, follow the paved path back to your car.

7 Grotto Falls

This three-mile round trip takes you not only *to* but *under* one of the park's few true falls. The trail also crosses several streams on stones, passes giant hemlocks and winds through tunnels of rhododendron and leucothoe. If you take this Walk late Monday, Wednesday or Friday afternoon between late March and mid-November you may pass a small pack train of llamas carrying supplies from LeConte Lodge (see Walk No. 20). Also, you drive to and from the trailhead on the five-mile-long Roaring Fork Motor Nature Trail, a narrow but paved one-lane road that takes you past a robust cascading stream and several interesting pioneer structures.

Grotto Falls is in the north-central part of the park, east of the Sugarlands Visitor Center. You get there from Gatlinburg. At traffic light number 8 on Route 441 (Gatlinburg's main street, also known as the Parkway) turn south onto Airport Road. In about half a mile you'll come to a four-way intersection. Take your right-most turn, which is Cherokee Orchard Road. In 3.2 miles you'll come to the Roaring Fork Motor Nature Trail. In a metal box beside the road pick up the 16-page, full-color brochure that explains the history of Roaring Fork's 19th-century pioneer community, as well as its historic cemetery, tub mill, farmhouses and other buildings you'll see on the way. The brochure also describes the views, the trees and the many other impressive natural features you'll

Llamas, which carry supplies to LeConte Lodge on Mount LeConte, pause in front of **Grotto Falls** *(Walk No. 7).* ▶

see from the road.

The nature trail winds up the steep slope of Piney Mountain, past thick stands of rhododendrons and several overlooks (described in the brochure). About 1.7 miles from its beginning, the trail reaches stop number 5, which is the Grotto Falls trailhead. Park on the left side of the road. The trail starts on the right side of the road, opposite the northern end of the parking area.

The popular trail is wide, well worn and, except for some small roots, relatively smooth. It passes through a shadowy forest of mostly large hemlocks. Huge, moss-covered logs, the corpses of ancient trees, lie rotting beside the trail. Rhododendrons, leucothoe and the tiny, shiny green leaves and red berries of partridgeberry grow between them.

You barely begin your walk before you hear—but at first cannot see—a stream to your left. It's one of four you'll cross as you gently traverse the steep slope of Piney Mountain. All four creeks flow down the ravines in the creases of the hillside. In every crossing the trail follows the creek briefly upstream as it gently drops into the streambed, which is always thick with moisture-loving rhododendrons and leucothoe and sometimes jewelweed. After crossing the creek, the trail switches back and heads downstream as it gently climbs away from the stream, up the slope of the ravine and over the next ridge before it gradually descends another ridge, winds down to a stream and does the same things all over again.

After crossing the fourth creek, the trail enters a thick tunnel of rhododendrons and leucothoe. Suddenly you hear the loud sound of water on your left. Then you see Roaring Fork at the bottom of a ravine. Your views of the creek get better as you get closer to it and follow it upstream. Soon you glimpse Grotto Falls a few hundred feet ahead. As the creek plunges over its rock-choked bed in dozens of tiny falls you pass through large, dense rhododendrons and leucothoe growing out of huge, moss-covered logs. Soon you're beside the 25-foot-long pool that spans the width of the 15-foot-wide creek bed in front of the falls.

Unlike most Smoky Mountain falls, the ledge wall over which Grotto drops isn't convex—it doesn't curve outward toward the direction of the falls—so Grotto Falls doesn't cascade or slide across a rock face. Instead, Grotto's ledge is concave—it curves inward, like a cave or grotto, away from the direction of the falls—so Grotto Falls doesn't run down a ledge but, instead, drops over the edge of one and falls freely for 20 feet, without striking anything, until it splashes on more ledge at the edge of the pool below. Grotto is what purists call a true falls.

And you can walk underneath it without getting drenched. The mouth of the moist, mossy "grotto" behind the falls is 40 feet wide and 20 feet deep at its deepest point. The grotto is only six feet deep where the creek falls in front of it but that gives you plenty of room to slip behind the curtain of water. Stay close to the ledge if you want to stay dry. On the other hand, if it's a warm day you might be tempted to stick your hands and even your face in the falls and enjoy a quick, cold natural shower.

Whatever you do at the falls, be sure you enjoy not only the falling water but also the view of the lush, steep-sided

Midnight Hole, a large, emerald pool on Big Creek, seen on the trail to **Mouse Creek Falls** *(Walk No. 8).* ▶

ravine, which is green with rhododendrons, leucothoe and giant trees and sparkling with churning white water.

When you're ready, turn around and walk back to your car.

If you're on the trail an hour or so before dark on a Monday, Wednesday or Friday afternoon between late March and mid-November you may see a train of half a dozen or so llamas coming down from LeConte Lodge. Llamas are small, graceful, patient pack animals. The most common word used to describe them, it seems, is "cute." The lodge uses them instead of horses to carry supplies because llamas' padded feet (unlike horses' hoofs) do virtually no harm to the trails.

After you reach your car you drive the rest of the Roaring Fork Motor Nature Trail back to Gatlinburg. You'll go through the forest down Piney Mountain and along exciting, cascading Roaring Fork. You'll also pass the trail's historic structures and, near the end of the trail on your left, the waterfalls called "The Place of a Thousand Drips." The trail exits the park and reenters Gatlinburg on Roaring Fork Road, which keeps following Roaring Fork closely until the road ends at Route 73 (also known as East Parkway) less than half a mile north of traffic light number 3 on Route 441.

8 Mouse Creek Falls

Forty-foot-high **Mouse Creek Falls** *(Walk No. 8) is part of one of the most engrossing displays of moving water in the Smokies.*

◀

This four-mile round trip takes you not only to one of the most exciting cascades in the park but also to a fascinating surreal formation known as the Rock House; a beautiful wide, deep, green trout pool known as Midnight Hole; and a large cascading stream, which not for nothing is called Big Creek.

The Walk is in the northeastern edge of the park, about 35 miles from Gatlinburg. The drive there from Gatlinburg is especially scenic. Take Route 321 to Cosby, then Route 321 and 32 1.9 miles north to the Foothills Parkway.

The parkway is only six miles long but it has four scenic overlooks—at 1.6, 2.3, 3.8 and 4.9 miles. The first two, on the right, are dramatic. Below you are the smooth green fields in the valley around Cosby. Beyond the fields are heavily forested, sharply creased mountains—some of the highest peaks in the east, rising thousands of feet above the valley. You see not only Gabes and Round mountains and other, lower summits but also 4,928-foot-high Mount Cammerer and other points along the Smokies' long, mile-high crest. The last two overlooks, on the left, show you the mountains, fields and picturesque weathered barns of the Great Valley of the Tennessee River.

At the end of the parkway head east on Interstate 40, which winds up the steep, narrow valley of the Pigeon River through the Cherokee National Forest. You'll see more views of the Smokies crest on your right and steep rock outcrops on your left.

About 7.3 miles from the parkway take the Waterville Road exit (number 451). The exit ramp ends at a stop sign just before a bridge over the Pigeon River. Cross the bridge, take a left and follow the river upstream. In 1.3 miles you'll cross the Tennessee-North Carolina state line and pass a brick hydroelectric power plant owned by the Carolina Power and Light Co. After another .9 miles you'll come to a four-way intersection at the boundary of the national park. Go straight ahead. The road immediately becomes gravel and, .2 miles from the intersection, passes the Big Creek ranger station, on the right. In another .7 miles the road makes a 90-degree turn to the left. The beginning of the Big Creek Trail is at the bend in the road on your right. There's a small parking area in front of the trailhead.

The Big Creek Trail is an old railroad bed, which means it's gently graded and very wide. However, it's slightly rocky in places — especially upstream — so hiking boots are a good idea.

The trail begins by gently climbing the steep lower slope of Mount Cammerer. The forest rises sharply on your right and drops steeply on your left. Through the open woods on the left you can see deep into the Big Creek valley and across to the ridges of Mount Sterling rising up the other side. Drifts of wild asters and lady fingers grow on both sides of the trail.

Soon you hear, and a bit later you see, Big Creek roaring over its rocky bed more than 50 feet below the trail.

Then you come to a fascinating jumble of huge rocks scattered on the right side of the trail as far up the steep hillside as you can see. Here the rocks actually outnumber the trees. The woods are a forest not of hemlock or poplar but of sandstone.

As the trail gets closer to the creek, you'll see rocks spread thickly on *both* sides of the trail. At this point, a bit more than a mile from the trailhead, look carefully for the Rock House. This is an especially large boulder — as big as a small two-story house — about 200 feet up the hill on the right side of the trail. Carved out of a corner of this boulder is a 20-foot-high, 14-by-18 foot "room" whose ceiling and two walls are not only remarkably flat but also nearly perpendicular to each other, as if they were man-made. The room looks a bit like the foyer of a modern office building. It's said that, long ago, people actually lived in the Rock House. It's certainly one of the best natural shelters you could find in the Smokies. In its inside corner you could probably stay dry in a rainstorm. Unfortunately there's no sign for the Rock House and the trail to it is steep, rocky and hard to find (though also mercifully short). The best advice we can give is: Look for the rock that looks like the Rock House and look for what looks like the easiest way to walk to it. You'll probably find both the Rock House and the path leading to it.

After passing the Rock House, the Big Creek Trail stays close to the stream. Now you can see how the creek earns its name. It's 30 to 40 feet wide, sometimes two or three feet deep and bristling with noisy falls, cascades and rapids. It's one of the most exciting creeks in the Smokies.

You'll soon come to one of the creek's most beautiful features: a large, deep, emerald-green pool known as Midnight Hole. You'll see it on your left, about 30 feet before you come to a horse-hitching bar on your right. Stone steps take you down the low stone embankment on the left side of the trail and more stone steps lead to the rocky edge of the 30-by-50-foot pool. Cabin-size boulders dam the creek on the upstream side of the pool. They also compress the stream into two narrow channels and force it into thick, white surging bottlenecks of water before it plunges deep into the green pool. The mixture of white and green water on the far side of the pool looks like a creme de menthe parfait. Near the falls the pool is aqua-colored. Farther away it's darker green and near its edge it's darker still. Though the pool is more than 12 feet deep in places, the water is so clear you can see all the way to the bottom. You can watch trout drifting in the current as the water moves slowly counterclockwise, away from the falls, then back. Huge rhododendrons grow among the boulders and ledges all around the edge of the green water.

If you want to see the turbulent creek at the head of the falls, walk a few feet more up the trail, then carefully pick your way through the rhododendrons and across the rocks to the stream. You'll see long, shallow pools and a knot of minifalls above them. From here you can work your way downstream, over the boulders and the long, smooth ledges that enter the pool like beaches made of stone instead of sand. The roar of the falls is so loud that conversation here is impossible. The overwhelming scale of this place — the result of raging water, huge rocks and giant rhododendrons — makes it not only beautiful but stirring enough to be sublime.

After Midnight Hole the Big Creek Trail passes through more thickets of rhododendrons and leucothoe and offers still more views of the cascading creek. Then, about two miles from the trailhead, you'll come to another horse-hitching rail on your left and a wooden sign saying "Mouse Creek Falls." You can see the falls from a log bench at the top of the creek bank about 30 feet from the trail. But for your best view climb carefully down the bank to the creek.

There you'll be in the middle of one of the loudest, liveliest, most engrossing displays of moving water in the Smokies. Ahead of you, on the opposite side of Big Creek, are Mouse Creek Falls. Like Toms Branch Falls (Walk No. 4) and Huskey Branch Cascades (Walk No. 5), Mouse Creek Falls are created when the creek on which they're found and after which they're named tumbles over a ledge as it flows into another stream.

Like Toms Branch Falls, Mouse Creek Falls are wonderfully complex. They begin when two streams of water flow over the top of a 40-foot-high ledge and run toward each other until they meet in a 12-foot-long hollow in the rock. The stream on your right is modest but the one on your left is big. It flows down the ledge in four different falls, each one two to four feet high and slighter narrower than the one above it.

Then the falling water runs out of the hollow and proceeds down the ledge in an elaborate tapestry of rock and water. Some of the water drops 12 feet to a shelf in the ledge. Some of it falls closer to the ledge, dropping in two dozen tiny falls and cascades.

After sliding over the face of the ledge, the falls tumble over a craggy 12-foot-high section of the moss-covered rock and create one last, tiny fall at the bottom of the ledge before entering Big Creek.

Mouse Creek Falls, however, are only part of the excitement. Big Creek, running below and perpendicular to Mouse Creek, provides the rest. In all you have a 180-degree view of white water, a circus of cascading streams, one of the largest, widest water vistas in the Smokies. Upstream, for example, a series of wide, foot-high cascades divides the creek into more than a dozen small water terraces. Just to your right a three-foot-high cascade plunges into an aqua pool and frothy white foam bubbles to the surface. Downstream a thick, gleaming slab of water runs into a 20-foot-long pool that spans the 40-foot-wide creek. The falling water creates a white column of foam that churns in the clear pool.

You can stand here for a long time contemplating the many ways that water moves over rocks: sometimes plunging over them in white falls, sometimes sliding over them in thin, transparent films. You can also watch how water moves between rocks: smoothly, softly, quietly when there's plenty of room; in a noisy, snow-colored surge when a yard of water is trying to squeeze through one foot of space.

Not surprisingly, Mouse Creek Falls is the highlight of the Walk. Big Creek, however, remains lively and the trail beside it remains nearly level for the next several miles. Just .2 miles ahead, for example, a bridge crosses the stream beside a large, still pool bordered by large boulders and, upstream from the bridge, dozens of tiny falls create a luscious stretch of white water.

However far you decide to walk, you can enjoy the views of Big Creek all over again, from an upstream perspective, when you retrace your steps to your car.

9 Henwallow Falls

This undemanding four-mile round trip features two things. One is 40-foot-high Henwallow Falls, which splatters leisurely down a dark, mossy ledge framed by rhododendrons. The other is a classic Smokies landscape: a moist, lush forest of towering rhododendrons, huge hemlocks and big, moss-covered trunks of fallen trees, a place so wet you cross five creeks in less than three-quarters of a mile and so damp that the half-log bridges over the creeks are slippery even on dry days.

The Walk begins in Cosby Campground, in the northeast section of the park. To get there from Gatlinburg take Route 321 to Cosby. In Cosby go right on Route 32. In 1.2 miles take another right onto the road to Cosby Campground. The Gabes Mountain Trail, which goes to Henwallow Falls, is two miles ahead on the right. Leave your car in the hikers' parking lot, a few hundred feet beyond the trailhead on the left.

At first the Gabes Mountain Trail climbs gently up through a mixed forest of hardwoods and hemlocks, rhododendrons and partridgeberry. Soon you can hear, and a few minutes later you can see, rhododendron-lined Rock Creek on your right. You'll agree that the cascading stream is well named.

Just .3 miles from the trailhead the trail splits. The path on the left leads to Cosby Campground. The one on the right goes to the falls.

Immediately after the trail junction you cross Rock Creek on a wide, half-log bridge. (Watch your step and hold on to the hand railing because the log may be wet.) Upstream from the bridge you can see the creek tumbling over large, smooth rocks in dozens of tiny falls.

The trail is now virtually level as it winds through a junglelike forest of towering two- and three-foot-thick hemlocks, huge, moss-covered trunks of fallen trees and thick patches of 12-foot-tall rosebay rhododendrons. So dense are the rhododendrons, so lush is the setting that you feel as if you're strolling through an immense conservatory.

You soon cross another, tiny creek on stones, then two more creeks on half-log bridges.

The trail then climbs a bit and you come to a fifth creek, crowded with rhododendrons, which you cross on a stone bridge. The last four streams, incidentally, are all tributaries of Crying Creek, named after a man who accidentally shot his brother while the two of them were hunting.

About a mile from the trailhead the path meets an old logging road. A trail marker here says the falls is 1.2 miles ahead.

The trail then climbs gently through a grove of young hemlocks, passes through a tunnel of rhododendrons and runs across a slope, which rises steeply on the left and drops sharply on the right.

Then the trail descends to a tiny creek, thick with rhododendrons. After crossing it on another stone bridge the path weaves in and out of rhododendron thickets as it starts climbing across the steep slope of Gabes Mountain. The mountain again rises steeply on

Forty-foot-high **Henwallow Falls** _(Walk No. 9) splatters down a dark, mossy ledge._ ▶

the left and falls off to your right.

You cross another tiny stream trickling down through large rocks on your left and then pass massive jagged, moss-covered rock outcrops rising high above the trail.

Finally, two miles from the trailhead, you come to another trail junction. The Gabes Mountain Trail goes straight ahead and, in a few hundred feet, crosses tiny Henwallow Creek, after which the falls are named. You can't see any falls from here, however, and both the view of the creek and the view through the trees of the Cosby valley are unremarkable. So instead of going straight ahead on the Gabes Mountain Trail at the intersection, we suggest you take the .1-mile-long side trail to the right, which immediately starts switching back and forth, through hemlocks and rhododendrons, down the steep slope of the mountain until it stops at the jumble of boulders at the base of Henwallow Falls.

The falls begin in a two-foot-wide stream that pours over the top of a 50-foot-high ledge. The stream dribbles and splatters down the face of the ledge, fanning out wider and wider until, when it reaches the bottom, it's a thin sheet of water spread 25 feet across the dark, mossy ledge. So gentle is the falls that moss grows almost all over the ledge. The moss is green where it escapes the water, on both sides of the falls, but it looks almost black where it's soaking wet underneath the transparent sheet of water.

When you're ready, head back to your car and enjoy the lush woodland garden of hemlocks and rhododendrons all over again.

10 Abrams Falls

This relatively easy five-mile round trip takes you along Abrams Creek to 20-foot-high Abrams Falls and the deep, 60-foot-wide pool below it, which is one of the largest in the Smokies.

The Abrams Falls Trail begins in Cades Cove, in the northwestern part of the park. To get to the trailhead, follow the Cades Cove Loop Road to the western end of the cove. (Allow as much as half an hour for that 5.5-mile trip because the Cove is a popular destination and traffic often moves very slowly along the one-lane, one-way road.) Immediately after crossing Abrams Creek take a right onto the short gravel road that leads to the trailhead parking lot.

Enter the woods at the western end of the parking area and cross a large footbridge over Abrams Creek. Take a left at the fork on the other side of the creek and follow the trail through a thick tunnel of rosebay rhododendrons, some of which are 20 feet high.

The wide, smooth trail stays near Abrams Creek as it follows the shallow, 30-foot-wide river downstream toward the falls. Unlike other Smoky Mountain creeks, Abrams flows smoothly here, with only small cataracts as it drops over mossy ledges stretching across the stream. You catch many glimpses of the creek through the rhododendrons growing along its banks and several short paths take you to the edge of the stream for closer looks. And while you don't always see the stream you almost always hear it.

Soon the trail climbs a low rise, temporarily moving away from the creek. Then it gradually descends and returns to the creek before crossing Arbutus Branch, a tributary of Abrams Creek, on a half-log bridge.

After following the creek awhile the trail climbs up and away from it again and passes through a dry woods of pines and mountain laurel. Then, about a mile from the trailhead, the path dramatically switches back to the right in the middle of a jagged ledge at a tiny pass at the top of Arbutus Ridge. From there the trail gradually descends back to the creek, which is now rockier and noisier. You see more cascades and more white water.

The trail then crosses another small tributary and passes clusters of galax, whose shiny dark green, not-quite-round-but-not-quite-square leaves grow only two to four inches off the ground.

Then the trail crosses another tributary, Stony Branch, on another half-log bridge and immediately after comes to a small beach beside the creek. Abrams Creek is about 50 feet across here and, as it flows in tiny falls over wide ledges, it creates some of the widest falls in the park.

After following the creek for a bit the trail climbs gently up a third rise. Here dense patches of mountain laurel replace rhododendrons in the drier soil. At the crest of the rise, you briefly hear the loud noise of the falls on your left. Rhododendrons reappear (and

Road Prong flows through a parklike setting at the beginning of the **Chimney Tops Trail** *(Walk No. 12).* ▶

mountain laurel disappears) as you climb back down toward the creek.

Soon the trail comes to another tributary, Wilson Branch, which flows over long, wide, smooth ledges. You cross the creek on a half-log bridge, follow it briefly downstream through thick rhododendrons and cross it again on another half-log bridge. You're now beside Abrams Creek again and Abrams Falls is straight ahead of you.

This 25-foot-high cataract is created the same way that the many smaller falls you saw upstream are created: by a ledge that spans the creek, forming a natural dam that the creek has no choice but to fall over. Abrams Falls is unique because the ledge *it* falls over is 25 feet high.

Unlike, say, Mouse Creek Falls, Abrams is simple. It drops over its ledge in two broad streams, bounces on a rock shelf about one third of the way down, then falls in a single 20-foot-wide apron of water into the pond-size pool below.

After you've enjoyed the falls — and perhaps a picnic lunch — follow the trail back to your car.

Abrams Falls and Abrams Creek, incidentally, are named after Old Abram, the chief of the Cherokee Indian village of Chilhowee, which once stood near the mouth of the creek. Abram and several other Cherokee chiefs were murdered by a 17-year-old white boy to avenge the massacre of his family — by Creek Indians, not Cherokees. According to legend he split open their skulls with an ax.

11 Rainbow Falls

This 5.4-mile round trip takes you up the slope of Mount LeConte, past giant rocks and huge trees, to Rainbow Falls, the highest true falls in the park. Rainbow is a diaphanous curtain of water that falls 80 feet over an enormous concave ledge. When the sun hits the falls in the afternoon you can see rainbows in the misty water.

The trail to the falls climbs 1,750 feet in 2.7 miles—a rate of about 648 feet per mile. That climb makes this Walk one of the most demanding Great Walk in the Smokies. It's not arduous but it *is* a long steady climb. The Walk will be easier for you if you get in shape on the other, gentler Walks first and if you allow yourself enough time to do this one slowly.

Like Grotto Falls, Rainbow Falls is in the north-central part of the park, east of the Sugarlands Visitor Center, and you get there from Gatlinburg. If you're on Route 441 (also known as the Parkway) in downtown Gatlinburg, turn south onto Airport Road at traffic light number 8. In about half a mile you'll come to a four-way intersection, where you turn right onto Cherokee Orchard Road. In 2.5 miles you'll come to the trailhead parking area, on the right. The trail begins in the southwest corner of the parking lot.

You'll walk barely .1 miles on a wide, well-worn path before you pass the beginning of the Trillium Gap Trail on your left. Then you'll enter a forest of huge hemlocks and hardwoods. You'll see large clusters of rocks and three-foot-thick trunks of fallen trees, many of them hollow, on both sides of the trail. The path roughly parallels LeConte Creek, on the right, and you can often hear and occasionally see the rocky, rushing stream. The trail is often pleasantly cobbled with low, rounded rocks. So as you climb past large rosebay rhododendrons you sometimes feel as if you're walking through a woodland rock garden.

As the trail climbs up the mountain, you slowly move away from the creek and you get views of Cove Mountain and other low summits through the trees behind you and to your left.

After almost a mile from the trailhead the path switches back to the right and briefly passes through a dry forest of pine and mountain laurel. Here the mountain views are on your right and straight ahead.

Then the trail passes through a long tunnel of both laurel and rhododendrons before crossing LeConte Creek on a half-log bridge. Upstream you see three- and four-foot-high cascades as the creek tumbles over a jumble of rocks as big as Volkswagen Beetles.

In a few minutes the trail switches back to the left at a giant five-foot-thick hemlock. You can now see the slope of Rocky Spur to your left.

Next you come to a tributary of LeConte Creek on your left. You cross this small stream on rocks in front of a 40-foot-wide ledge that stretches across the creek like a dam. From the top of the ledge a delicate trickle of

The John Oliver Cabin is one of nearly two dozen 19th-century buildings you can see in **Cades Cove** *(Walk No. 16).*　▶

water falls eight feet to the creek below. It looks and sounds like rainwater falling off a roof.

The mountain views through the trees continue as the trail crosses another small creek on rocks and another tiny falls — this one 12 feet high — dribbles over the top of a ledge across the stream bed to your right.

Finally, the trail crosses LeConte Creek for the second time. Look upstream from the half-log bridge and you'll catch your first glimpse of Rainbow Falls, just a few hundred feet away.

The trail follows the cascading, boulder-filled creek upstream to another bridge at the base of the falls. In front of you will be a gigantic, 120-foot-wide, 80-foot-high concave ledge that spreads across LeConte Creek like a huge, rough movie screen. A thin sheet of water falls over the top of the ledge and drops freely for almost 60 feet before it splatters on a slope of the ledge below, creating a fine spray that can be felt 20 feet away. Then the stream slides ten feet down the moss-covered rock in a wide, thin sheet of water.

On sunny afternoons you can usually see a rainbow on the falls. Change your position and you can see the rainbow move up or down the shimmering white curtain of water.

The ledge behind the falls is fascinating too. Note how the striations in the rock slope downward from each end of the ledge toward the center, making the cavelike ledge look even taller and deeper than it is. Also notice the hemlocks and other trees growing along the sides of the ledge, the rhododendrons on top of it and the long shelf of smaller plants just below the top.

If you'd like to see another charming rock-and-water feature, keep following the Rainbow Falls Trail beyond

LeConte Creek for less than .1 mile. After passing through lush growths of leucothoe, rhododendrons and hemlocks the trail bends sharply to the right. Here, on your left, water flows delightfully along the creases of a mossy ledge before running across the path in front of you. This charming natural fountain isn't as spectacular as Rainbow Falls but it's every bit as memorable.

When you're ready to go back to your car, simply retrace your steps to the parking lot. Needless to say, you'll find the walk down easier than the walk up.

12 Chimney Tops Trail

This .8-mile round trip is one of the shortest, easiest and most beautiful Walks in the Smokies. You'll stroll on a wide, smooth trail through a lush, green parklike setting of giant hemlocks, huge, moss-covered fallen trees and dense stands of rosebay rhododendrons. You'll also cross two large cascading mountain streams on three different bridges that are perfect platforms from which to enjoy the rushing white water.

The Chimney Tops Trail begins at a paved parking area on the Newfound Gap Road, about seven miles south of the Sugarlands Visitor Center and about six miles north of Newfound Gap. Signs indicate that the two-mile trail ultimately leads to the twin pointed ledges on a knob of Sugarland Mountain known as the Chimney Tops. The view from the Chimney Tops is panoramic but much of the last 1.5 miles of the trail to the top is a stiff climb and it includes a long, steep, straight section that's especially unpleasant. But if the last three quarters of the trail are too steep to be a Great Walk, the first quarter is definitely not.

You begin this Walk by climbing down handsome stone steps and then following a rail fence as the wide, smooth path starts winding gently down to the West Prong of the Little Pigeon River. The trail passes under giant hemlocks and beside immense, moss-covered trunks of dead trees decaying on the forest floor. Rhododendrons grow as much as 12 feet tall in the moist shade.

The trail quickly crosses the West Prong — one of the park's largest streams — on a footbridge. Below you, upstream and down, the 50-foot-wide river surges noisily over large rocks. On both sides of the creek rhododendrons grow in an impressive monoculture unblemished by the intrusion of any other shrub. Suddenly you realize you're standing in a splendid evergreen garden whose focal point is a rocky white-water stream and which, like many great gardens, is composed of just a few species and just a few colors: the dark green of the hemlocks, the moss and the rhododendrons; the gray of the rocks and the still water; and the pure white of the cascading water.

The water-powered John Cable Mill in **Cades Cove** *(Walk No. 16) still grinds corn into cornmeal. Leaning out the window is Hubert Sullivan of the Great Smoky Mountains Natural History Association, who operates the mill and tells visitors how it works.* ▶

You barely cross the West Prong when you cross another creek, Road Prong, just before it rushes into the West Prong about 100 feet below the West Prong bridge. Road Prong is a quieter stream than the West Prong. Rather than churning over boulders it flows more softly over small rocks and wide, mossy ledges that stretch across the creek. Upstream from the second bridge, a ledge creates a natural dam and a four-foot-high waterfall flows over it. The stream is framed on both banks by solid thickets of rhododendrons. You think to yourself: This section of woodland stream looks as good as a very good woodland garden.

After crossing Road Prong, the trail splits. The right fork goes down, past hemlocks and rhododendrons, to the West Prong. The left fork follows Road Prong upstream. Although the trail climbs above the creek, you still catch glimpses of it. From the wide, smooth, nearly level trail you also see large hemlocks and hardwoods and solid drifts of rhododendrons that stretch up and down the slopes on both sides of the trail for as far as you can see.

Less than .4 miles from the trailhead you come to the second bridge over Road Prong. Walk onto the bridge and enjoy the upstream view of the wide, rock-filled stream punctuated by dozens of tiny falls and cascades.

When you're ready, turn around and enjoy this natural park from another perspective as you retrace your steps to your car.

13 Mingus Mill

Barely .2 miles long, this pleasant and interesting stroll is the shortest and easiest Great Walk in the park. It brings you to a water-powered 19th-century gristmill, where you can watch corn being ground into cornmeal, and takes you (for a change) along two *man-made* streams: the elevated, 130-foot-long wooden flume and the 200-foot-long race that carry water from Mingus Creek to the 2¹/₂-story wooden mill.

This Walk is on the Newfound Gap Road, about half a mile north of the Oconaluftee Visitor Center. Brown-and-white park signs direct you to a paved parking area just off the highway.

From the south side of the parking lot, paved walkways take you quickly to a wooden bridge over Mingus Creek. You'll see the mill on your right just after you cross the rhododendron-lined stream. You'll also see, just ahead of you, a box containing *Mingus Mill Self-guiding Trail* pamphlets. This brochure describes the history of the century-old mill and explains how, with the help of Mingus Creek, it turns corn into cornmeal.

Be sure to tour the inside of the mill, which is operated by the Great Smoky Mountains Natural History Association and open daily from mid-April through October. Association interpreters will enthusiastically answer any questions you might have.

Outside the mill you can walk upstream along Mingus Creek and along the 130-foot-long flume, a long wooden aquaduct supported by log cribs, some of which are almost 20 feet high. The flume carries a stream of water as big as a small creek to the top of a 22-

foot-high penstock beside the mill. The pressure of the water falling down the penstock turns a cast-iron turbine that provides all the mill's power.

So much water flows through the flume that some of it must be let out before it reaches the mill. The result is an exciting man-made waterfall that plunges 18 feet from the top of the flume to the ground beneath it.

Keep walking upstream, past the flume, and you'll come to the race. This is an elegant, one-foot-deep, three- to four-foot-wide and 200-foot-long canal that carries water along the shady bottom of a hill from Mingus Creek to the flume. Moss and tiny rhododendrons grow out of the soaking wet boards that form the walls of the race. Inside, three or four inches of water move briskly along toward the flume.

The race ends at Mingus Creek, where a small dam diverts water into the structure. Turn around here and enjoy a second look at the mill and its manmade streams as you walk back to your car.

14 The Noah "Bud" Ogle Place

This easy Walk is only three-quarters of a mile long but it takes you to many interesting things:

Charlies Bunyon (*Walk No. 19*) *rises from the Smokies' crest like the ruins of an ancient castle.*

◄

the rough, century-old two-room cabin that was home for "Bud" Ogle, his wife Cindy and their large family; the 50-foot-long flume that still carries "running water" to the porch of their cabin; another, 100-foot-long flume that still carries water to the Ogles' "tub" mill on LeConte Creek; and a quintessential Great Smokies creekside landscape that's so moist that you cross seven different streams in just a few hundred feet and so thick with giant rhododendrons, hemlocks and other trees that it was once called Junglebrook.

Like Grotto Falls (Walk No. 7) and Rainbow Falls (Walk No. 11), the Ogle Place is in the north-central part of the park and you get there from Gatlinburg. If you're on Route 441 (the Parkway) turn south onto Airport Road at traffic light number 8. In half a mile you'll come to a four-way intersection, where you turn right onto Cherokee Orchard Road. The Ogle Place parking area is two miles ahead on the right.

Pick up the *Self-guiding Nature Trail* pamphlet in a box by the trailhead at the southern edge of the parking area. The brochure, published by the Great Smoky Mountains Natural History Association, explains the man-made and natural features you'll see on the Walk. It tells how a nearly self-sufficient family like the Ogles lived and how almost all their food and shelter came from the land you'll be walking on.

Follow the trail down from the parking area, across a creek and toward the Ogle cabin. After the trail's first numbered stop, which is just before the cabin, the path turns right and goes along the short, northern side of the house (the one facing the parking area). Take a minute or two to tour the cabin. And be sure to look at the 50-foot-long wooden flume that still carries water from a spring to a double sink beside the porch that's carved out of just one large log.

When you're ready to continue the Walk, return to the trail at the north side of the cabin and follow it into the woods. After crossing another small creek on large flat rocks you'll cross still another, larger stream on a bridge made out of a large log. Then you'll pass through a thicket of rhododendrons and a grove of giant hemlocks. Next you'll see the stone walls of a former pasture and then the stone remains of a "weaner" cabin. This cabin was where each of the Ogles' newly married sons was allowed to live with his wife for one year while the couple was establishing its own farm. Also look for the tall boxwood plants growing in rows to the left of the trail. They're reminders that, after the Ogles sold the property and before it became part of the park, the land was used to grow nursery stock.

By now you can hear LeConte Creek. In just a minute you'll be at the banks of the loudly cascading stream and the restored Ogle tubmill, so called because it used a tub or basin to catch the water that powered the gristmill. Unlike the Mingus Mill (Walk No. 13) and the John Cable Mill in Cades Cove (Walk No. 16), the Ogle Mill no longer operates. But a 100-foot-long wooden flume still carries water from the creek to the 12-by-12-foot millhouse. The flume begins at the bottom of a dam that's made out of one large log. The dam creates a one-foot-high, 30-foot-long waterfall that stretches all the way across the creek. Parts of the flume have started to rot and they provide a rich, moist habitat for thick green moss.

The trail then follows the creek briefly upstream before heading back toward the Ogle house. It passes through a grove of huge hemlocks, skirts an 8-by-14-foot boulder and then, in just a few hundred feet, crosses seven small creeks (on logs or stones) as it winds among giant rosebay rhododendrons.

The trail emerges from the woods beside the Ogle barn, which, like almost all early Smoky Mountain farm buildings, is built of logs. Check out the inside of this 1½-story structure and note how large hollow logs made nifty feed troughs.

The barn is only about 150 feet from the Ogle house. From there you retrace your steps to your car.

15 Pioneer Farmstead & Oconaluftee River

At first glance, the dozen buildings spread across the Pioneer Farmstead look like a replica of a village. But the buildings actually represent the structures that just one nearly self-sufficient 19th-century family would have used to survive on the edge of civilization. The Pioneer Farmstead, located beside the Oconaluftee Visitor Center, is the most extensive collection of early farm buildings in any one place in the national park. It includes a house, barn, woodshed, meat house, outhouse, blacksmith shop, springhouse, apple house, chickenhouse, pigpen, sorghum mill, corncribs, bee gum stand and gardens. A 12-page pamphlet prepared by the Great Smoky Mountains Natural History Association explains how each structure was used to provide food, fuel and other services to the pioneer family.

Both the farmstead and the Oconaluftee Visitor Center are on the Newfound Gap Road, one mile north of the Cherokee Indian Reservation, on the southern edge of the park.

The stroll around the farmstead is only about .3 miles long. If you'd like a longer walk, follow the smooth, level Oconaluftee River Trail to the Oconaluftee River and enjoy a stroll or perhaps a picnic beside the wide, swift-flowing stream. The trail begins behind the visitor center, near the entrance to the farmstead. It crosses the field just south of the farmstead, enters the woods and immediately reaches the banks of the Oconaluftee. The trail stays parallel to the river until it reaches the Cherokee Reservation in another 1.4 miles. The trail's best feature, however, is its views of the river and those views are never better than they are where the trail first meets the river just a few hundred feet southeast of the visitor center.

Whether you visit the river or only the farmstead, you end this Walk by turning around and following the path back to your car.

16 Cades Cove

The Pioneer Farmstead (Walk No. 15) is a replica of one family's farm; Cades Cove is a preservation of an entire pioneer community. Much of the cove, and its wonderful mountain views, can be seen by car on the 11-mile-long Cades Cove Loop Road. But parts of the cove can be explored on three different Walks: a .5-mile loop trail to a log cabin, a short stroll to the John Cable gristmill and six other farm buildings, and a .5-mile self-guiding nature trail that explains the different qualities of seven kinds of trees and how Cades Cove's pioneer farmers made good use of every one of them.

Named, according to legend, after Kate, the wife of the Cherokee chief Abram, Cades Cove is a Smoky Mountain anomaly: a relatively flat, fertile valley (or "cove," as they say in Appalachia) in the middle of the mountains. It was home to more than 600 people, nearly all of them farmers, in the 19th century and to about 500 people just before the park was established in the late 1920s. Today you can ride around the edge of the cove on the paved loop road: The narrow one-lane road takes you to impressive views of mountains rising behind rolling fields and to nearly two dozen old buildings, including a gristmill that still grinds corn, three plain wooden churches (a Primitive Baptist, a Missionary Baptist and a Methodist), six log cabins, a frame farmhouse, a blacksmith shop, a sorghum mill and several other farm buildings, including barns, corncribs and smokehouses.

You can read more about all these structures and how they served the people of Cades Cove in the *Cades Cove Auto Tour*, an illustrated 24-page pamphlet published by the Great Smoky Mountains Natural History Association and for sale at the beginning of the loop road.

You get to Cades Cove, which is in the northwestern part of the park, on the Laurel Creek Road, which connects the Cades Cove Loop Road to the three-way intersection known as the Townsend "Y," seven miles to the east.

The first Walk—the half-mile loop trail to the John Oliver cabin—is the auto tour's third stop. The trail begins in a parking area 1.3 miles from the start of the loop road. The shady leg of the loop trail goes through the woods, past vast drifts of lady fingers. The other leg, roughly parallel to the first, goes through an open field just west of the woods. Both legs lead to the cabin, which is surrounded by zigzagging split-rail fences. You can see this rustic building from the road; it sits at the far end of the field, at the bottom of a forested hillside. The auto tour brochure will tell you how it and other primitive pioneer structures were made.

The next Walk—around the John Cable Mill and surrounding buildings—is at stop number 11, which is about halfway around the loop road and right beside the Cades Cove Visitor Center. The auto tour brochure describes the mill, blacksmith shop, smokehouse, corncrib, sorghum mill and barns, as well as the Gregg-Cable House, the most elaborate old dwelling still standing in the cove. An attendant at the still-operating water-powered mill can tell you how it grinds corn into cornmeal.

The half-mile Cades Cove Self-guiding Nature Trail is stop number 13 on the auto tour and about .5 miles from the visitor center. Leave your car in the parking area on the right side of the road, pick up the trail brochure in the box in front of you, start following the loop trail through the forest and learn, among other things, why the pioneers' cabins were built of yellow poplar, why sourwood is perfect for sled runners and why dogwood was used for the gear teeth of gristmills.

You're apt to see more deer in Cades Cove than anywhere else in the park. The last time we were on the nature trail it was near dusk — one of the best times to see deer — and three fawns walked to within 12 feet of us and then frolicked with each other while we watched.

17 Look Rock

This gentle one-mile round trip takes you up a wide, paved, gently graded trail to a 50-foot-high observation tower on the top of Chilhowee Mountain that offers panoramic views of the Smokies. This Walk makes an excellent end-of-day excursion because the trail is short, the view of the sunset is excellent and the paved path is relatively easy to negotiate when you walk back to your car after the sun goes down.

The trail to Look Rock Tower begins on the section of the Foothills Parkway that runs just outside of, and parallel to, the northwestern boundary of the park. The parkway is often on or very near the long crest of Chilhowee Mountain and overlooks along the way provide views of both the mountain and the deep valleys on both sides of the road.

The northern end of the parkway is on Route 321 in Miller Cove. You can get to 321 from Gatlinburg by taking the Little River Road west from the Sugarlands Visitor Center. When you reach the three-way intersection known as the Townsend "Y," go right to Townsend, where you get on Route 321. You can also get on Route 321 in Pigeon Forge, which is just north of Gatlinburg, and follow it through Wear Cove — a broad agricultural valley with views of the Smokies to the south — and finally to Townsend. The southern end of the Parkway is on Route 129 on Chilhowee Lake. You get to Route 129 from Cherokee by taking Route 19 west to Route 74 in Bryson City, then Route 28 all the way to Route 129.

The Look Rock parking area is about nine miles south of Route 321, on the east side of the road. At the southern end of the parking lot is a handsome stone overlook from which you can look down at Happy Valley and the Cherokee National Forest, 1,000 feet below, and at Chilhowee Lake, six miles to the southwest.

The asphalt trail to Look Rock begins on the west side of the parkway, just north of the parking area. The four-foot-wide trail climbs gently up the slope of Chilhowee Mountain through a pleasant, dry forest of mostly oaks and pines. Near the top of the mountain the trail runs perpendicularly into a paved road. Go left here and you'll quickly reach a white-painted concrete tower.

According to several exhibits at the base of the tower,

Look Rock is no ordinary promontory. Throughout the 19th and early 20th centuries, Chilhowee Mountain was the site of large resort hotels, one of which boasted in an advertisement that "the summit of Chilhowee" has "one of the most magnificent views in the United States, comprising some 50 or 60 miles of the Great Valley of the Tennessee." The last of the hotels burned in 1933, according to the exhibit, but "the tradition of Look Rock" continued: On Easter Sunday, "throngs toiled up the primitive trail" to see the view from the rock. Today's travelers are luckier than yesterday's. The trail up the mountain is no longer "primitive" and, as the exhibit also notes, travelers can see the view not just from Look Rock but from a combination "fire lookout and visitor observation tower" that was built on the rock in 1967.

The "visitor observation" part of the tower is like a giant treehouse. It's a round, 24-foot-wide concrete platform surrounded by the tops of oak trees rustling softly in the breeze. You reach this platform via three long concrete ramps that switch gently back and forth from the shady forest floor to the man-made summit 50 feet above it.

Illustrated signs attached to the low wall along the edge of the platform describe the view. To the north are fields, farms and small towns in the Great Valley of the Tennessee River. Close by to the southwest is the long ridge of Chilhowee Mountain. To the south is Happy Valley and the Cherokee National Forest. To the south and east are the major mountains of the Smokies; Clingmans Dome and Mount LeConte (see Walk No. 20) are in the distance. The ridges of the mountains recede toward the horizon like ocean waves. The nearest ridge is a dark green forest — you can make out some of the trees. The ridge behind it is blue-green, the next one is blue and each succeeding ridge is a slightly lighter blue than the one in front of it; the last ridge is so pale it's almost the color of the sky. Each ridge has its unique solid color and is easily distinguished from the ridge in front of it and the one behind it. The closer ridges of Chilhowee Mountain are elegantly parallel and, like the ridges of the higher Smokies, each has its own color. Late in the day, the closest one is green, the next one is darker green, the one after that is even darker, the fourth is blue-green and the fifth is blue.

The last time we were there the sun was an incandescent red disk as it set to the right of Chilhowee Mountain and the color of each Chilhowee ridge was changed to a slightly different shade of blue. For a few minutes the horizon was as subtle, as delicate and as beautiful as a Japanese ink wash.

It was dark when we walked back to the car. But the wide, paved trail was easy to follow and the now-downhill grade was easy (and quick) to walk.

18 Alum Cave Bluffs

This five-mile round trip is easily one of the half-dozen best Walks in the Smokies. It offers an easy stroll along the parklike rhododendron-covered banks of Alum Cave Creek. It takes you up winding stone steps through an unusual rock tunnel known as Arch Rock. It pauses at a clearing from which you can savor a nearly 360-degree view of some of the Smokies' most dramatic mountains. And it climaxes at what may be the most curious phenomenon in the region: the immense Alum Cave Bluffs, beneath which, in one of the wettest places in the United States, is a tiny desert. A pamphlet published by the Great Smoky Mountains Natural History Association, available at the trailhead, describes the trees, shrubs, animals and other things you'll see on the Walk. This trail is part of the two-day excursion up Mount LeConte (Walk No. 20).

The Alum Cave Trail is in the north-central part of the park. It begins on the Newfound Gap Road, almost nine miles south of the Sugarlands Visitor Center and about five miles north of Newfound Gap. The trailhead is between two large adjacent parking areas on the east side of the road. It's linked to both areas by very short paths.

Pick up the *Self-guiding Nature Trail* brochure in the box at the trailhead, read the interesting information about Alum Cave and LeConte Lodge (see Walk No. 20) on the trailhead signs, cross the wooden footbridge over Walker Camp Prong and enter one of the most impressive places in the Smokies. Like the first part of the Chimney Tops Trail (Walk No. 12), it's one of those rare wild areas that nature has made as beautiful as a woodland garden. You are in a natural park dominated by huge hemlocks and birches and large thickets of rhododendrons and leucothoe. Because this area was not clear cut by 20th-century logging companies some of the hemlocks here are 200 years old and more than three feet thick. They're as big and beautiful as trees in a park. The giant rosebay rhododendrons grow all by themselves in large, solid drifts, just as they would in a well-planned garden. Nothing else creeps in to clutter up the perfect simplicity. The path, too, is parklike: wide, smooth, well worn and well made. It's handsomely braced with low walls and wet spots are cobbled with fine rounded stones.

After crossing Walker Camp Prong the trail barely goes 200 feet before it crosses Alum Creek. The views from the bridges over both streams are striking: Both upstream and downstream the wide creeks flow through long tunnels of rhododendrons, which grow thickly on both banks and over the softly cascading water.

The trail follows Alum Creek closely for almost a mile. Views of the stream are not constant — the rhododendrons are too thick — but there are many openings in the evergreens, and short side paths take you very quickly to pleasant views of rocks and white water.

In about a mile the rhododendrons thin out and the trail starts to climb along another creek, the Styx Branch, which it crosses three times on log bridges. (Be sure to hold on to the handrails when you walk across.)

When you cross the third log bridge (about 1.3 miles from the trailhead) you are at the rounded, 14-foot-high arch-shaped entrance to what you will immediately recognize as Arch Rock. Inside the rock is a short, steeply sloping tunnel that was carved out of the stream-side ledge by centuries of erosion. It's about 15 feet high, between 15 and 20 feet wide and about 25 feet long, and its rock wall is impressively striated with parallel diagonal lines.

You enter Arch Rock and immediately start climbing through the tunnel on 46 stone steps. First the steps spiral gracefully to the left, following the curve of the tunnel. You feel as if you're walking up the steps of a dark stone tower of a medieval castle. There's a steel cable attached to the ledge on your left in case you need something to hold on to.

At the mouth of the tunnel the steps turn right and take you to a shelf of a rock outcrop. You've now climbed 30 feet above the Styx Branch. There's another steel cable attached to the ledge on your right if you need it.

From here the trail quickly crosses the Styx again on another log bridge and then starts climbing across a spur of Mount LeConte.

Soon the trail skirts the edge of a thicket of rhododendrons called Huggins Hell. (Mountain people called large rhododendron groves "hells" because their many strong and tangled branches made them "hell" to walk through.)

Then the trail crosses a stream bed on rocks. After a rain you'll probably find water here. But if you take this Walk during a dry period such as the fall, you may find a rare Smoky Mountain sight: a dry stream.

As the trail climbs higher you start to see, through the trees, 5,500-foot-high Anakeesta Ridge rising above Alum Creek, now on your left. Looking back, you catch glimpses of the Boulevard, the long ridge that runs between Mount LeConte and the Appalachian Trail (see Walk No. 20).

The views get better and better until, less than two miles from the trailhead, there are suddenly no trees beside the trail. There is only gray ledge and what in the southern Appalachians is called a "heath bald": a mountain clearing where striking ericaceous plants like catawba rhododendrons, little-leaf (or Carolina) rhododendrons, mountain laurel, sand myrtle and sometimes grasses grow, but trees do not.

Keep going a few feet more and you'll reach a rough rock outcrop that provides one of the best views in the Smokies. From this 4,500-foot-high mountain aerie, the slopes of LeConte drop precipitously into the valley of Alum Cave Creek, to your left, and into the valley of the West Prong of the Little Pigeon River, ahead of you. On the other side of these valleys a wide circle of mountains rises steeply all around you. Behind you is LeConte, at 6,593 feet the third highest peak in the park. To your left rear is the Boulevard, scarred by landslides that tore hundreds of trees off its steep, 6,000-foot-high slopes. To the right of the Boulevard is the long Anakeesta Ridge, which stretches to the valley of Walker Camp Prong. To the right of the ridge is 5,802-foot-high Mingus Mountain and, to its right, mile-high Sugarland Mountain. On a spur of Sugarland Mountain, just to the right of the valley of Road Prong, you can see the twin peaks of the Chimney Tops. Off to your right is the long, thin, steep-sided, sharply pointed rock outcrop of Peregrine Ridge. Look carefully at the ridge and you can see a tiny round hole near the top of the rock. That's the Eye of the Needle. Look carefully at *all* the hills around you and you'll see places that are a lighter green than the tree-covered slopes. These are more heath balds, also known as "laurel slicks," so called because their smooth evergreen leaves look wet even when they're dry. Below you, though out of sight, is the parking area where you left your car.

This view is worth savoring not only because it's beautiful but also because it illustrates a point about mountains and beauty. Too many people, when judging a view, confuse quality with quantity. They talk only about how *far* you can see, how *many* mountains are visible. But beauty, of course, isn't measured in miles or mountain counts. It's measured by how *clearly* you can see the mountains, by how *well shaped* they are, by how *well composed* the entire view is. You can't see more than three or four miles from this overlook and, technically, you can't see more than a few mountains. But all that's irrelevant. This view is moving because you're surrounded, almost embraced, by a close ring of high, steep ridges and mountains that sweep up dramatically from the semicircle of deep valleys at your feet.

When you're ready to continue, follow the trail through a 200-foot-long tunnel of laurel and rhododendrons and then along a ledgy shelf in the steep side of the mountain. To your left the slope drops precipitously. To your right it rises abruptly; cliffs loom as much as 100 feet over your head. There's a steel cable on your right, which you might need to hold on to if the trail is icy or wet. Since there are few trees to block your view you'll see almost continuous vistas of Peregrine Ridge and Mingus and Sugarland mountains on your

The North Carolina Smokies seen in the autumn from a clearing on the Appalachian Trail, which leads to **Charlies Bunion** *(Walk No. 19) and* **Mount LeConte** *(Walk No. 20).* ▶

left. These views continue all the way to Alum Cave Bluffs.

Less than 2.5 miles from the trailhead the trail climbs a flight of 22 log steps to bring you to the base of Alum Cave Bluffs. The bluffs are an enormous, 200-foot-long ledge that extends as much as 50 feet over the trail, like a very shallow cave; hence their name. Even more striking than the ledge is what's beneath it: nothing but dusty gravel in which absolutely nothing grows. The contrast is surreal: Surrounding the "cave" is one of the rainiest places in North America, teeming with wet forests. The inside of the cave, on the other hand, is like a set from *Lawrence of Arabia*, the Desert of the Smokies.

The desert is caused by several things, the most important of which, of course, is the fact that the floor of the cave gets virtually no rain. Second, the floor consists mainly of debris that has worn off the ledge above it. That debris contains no organic matter, which is necessary for plant growth. Third, the floor of the cave is trampled by thousands of feet every year. Is it any wonder that it's as bare as a well-worn path?

The cave is named for the tiny traces of alum, or potassium aluminum sulfate, that groundwater has washed out of the ledge and deposited on the interior surfaces of the cave. Before the Civil War the Epsom Salts Co. mined the alum but later abandoned the project because it was not cost effective. During the Civil War, however, several hundred men supposedly extracted saltpeter from the ledge for use in Confederate gunpowder.

After you've contemplated the cave, turn around, follow the Alum Cave Trail back to your car and enjoy the special pleasures of this Walk all over again.

19 Charlies Bunion

Like the Alum Cave Trail, this is one of the six best Great Walks in the Smokies. It's an 8.4-mile round trip — the longest one-day Walk in the Smokies — but the trail is smooth and gently graded. It follows one of the park's most scenic stretches of the famous Maine-to-Georgia Appalachian Trail. Because it runs along the mile-high crest of the Smokies it's one of the highest walks in the Eastern United States. It offers frequent views of both the North Carolina and Tennessee sides of the crest, including several vistas of Mount LeConte, the Chimney Tops and Anakeesta Ridge, and it ends at the most stunning viewpoint in the Smokies: the unforgettable Charlies Bunion.

The Walk begins near the center of the park, where the Newfound Gap Road crosses the crest of the Smokies at 5,048-foot-high Newfound Gap, about 14 miles south of the Sugarlands Visitor Center and about 16 miles north of the Oconaluftee Visitor Center. Leave your car in the parking lot on the North Carolina side of the Tennessee-North Carolina boundary, take a look at the views of Mount LeConte and Anakeesta Ridge on the Tennessee side of the Gap and the mountains and valleys in North Carolina and read the informative plaques and other exhibits. Then head for the trailhead, which is at the eastern end of the parking lot, just to the right of the large fieldstone monument that memorializes the dedication of the park. (Bathrooms, if you need them, are about 200 feet down a paved walkway just to the right of the trailhead.)

The trail starts climbing gently on the North Carolina side of the Smokies crest. Except for occasional roots and rocks, which you can easily step over, on or around, the trail is wide, smooth, well worn and gently graded. It passes briefly through a forest of birches and other hardwoods before reaching the spruce-and-fir forest typical of the Appalachian highlands. Here you will notice the handiwork of balsam woolly adelgids, which have killed many of the Smokies' fir trees. The insects can turn lovely, luxuriant evergreens into ugly, brown, naked, dead tree trunks. The silver lining on the adelgid cloud, however, is that the insects, by killing so much vegetation, also open up many mountain viewpoints. If you look past the skeletons of dead trees you can now see many vistas that you wouldn't have been able to see before. Through the trees to your right, for example, you can catch glimpses of the switchbacks in the Newfound Gap Road and the layers of sharply etched mountain ridges, each one of which is a slightly different hue of green or blue than the one before or after it.

In about a third of a mile the trail ever so gradually crosses the Smokies crest and then climbs along the Tennessee side of the ridge. Now the views are on your left. Through the trees and through occasional open-

Autumn hoarfrost on evergreen trees on the Boulevard Trail turns **Mount LeConte** *(Walk No. 20) into a winter wonderland.* ▶

ings in the forest you can see the deep notch of the valley of Walker Camp Prong, the route of the Newfound Gap Road. Left of the valley is the eastern slope of Sugarland Mountain and, on a shoulder of Sugarland, the twin rock peaks of the Chimney Tops. To the right of the valley is Anakeesta Ridge and, behind the ridge, the top of Mount LeConte. The steep, forested slopes of both the mountain and the ridge have been scarred by landslides. One large slide on Anakeesta Ridge shows what these hills are really made of: The slide tore the thin skin of soil and trees off the side of the ridge, leaving only bare gray ledge. Walk slowly along this part of the Walk to make sure you don't miss the best views.

In about 1.5 miles the trail gradually climbs back to the crest of the Smokies. Just before the trail levels off a 20-foot-path takes you to a small grassy clearing in a beech gap on the right side of the trail. "Beech gap" is Appalachian Mountain talk for a grove of beech trees growing (usually) in a gap (or saddle) on a mountain ridge. The clearing is a pleasant place for a rest and to enjoy open, 30-degree views of the beautiful receding ridges of the North Carolina Smokies. In the fall this view is framed by golden beech leaves.

By now you've climbed almost 700 feet at the relatively moderate rate of about 466 feet per mile. You have another 300 feet to climb but you'll barely notice it because you'll be walking on the wide and almost level ridge crest. In fact you'll be climbing so slowly that you'll walk about another 1.2 miles before you reach the high point of the Walk — about 6,000 feet — high on the slope of Mount Kephart.

Indeed, from the clearing at the beech gap the trail

actually descends slightly until, 1.7 miles from the trailhead, it reaches the Sweat Heifer Trail, which enters the Appalachian Trail on the right. On the way to this trail junction there are occasional views through the trees of Anakeesta Ridge and Mount LeConte on your left.

After passing the Sweat Heifer Trail junction the trail is either level or rises only slightly. Blackberry and hobblebush grow along both sides of the wide walkway. Through the trees beyond them you have occasional views on both sides of the crest.

In about 2.2 miles the trail climbs briefly on the North Carolina side of the crest, past open views of the southern Smokies.

In about 2.7 miles the trail splits. The Boulevard Trail to the Jumpoff and Mount LeConte goes to the left. The Appalachian Trail goes right. The three-quarter-mile walk to the Jumpoff is rough, rocky, narrow and sometimes steep and its one view — into the deep valley northeast of the Boulevard and northwest of Charlies Bunion — is not as good as the many vistas at and around the Bunion. It is, however, one of the better views in the park. So if you have the time and don't mind the not-so-great walk to get there, go have a look. If, on the other hand, you want to go directly to the Bunion, take a right at the trail junction.

The trail to the Bunion now descends gradually along the North Carolina side of the Smokies' crest. You can see mountains through the trees on your right. In about half a mile you pass the fieldstone Ice Water Spring Shelter, one of 18 trail shelters in the park, 13 of which are along the popular Appalachian Trail. The amenities here are basic: a stone fireplace and two wooden sleeping platforms inside the shelter, a fire ring outside and a pit toilet nearby. Just beyond the shelter, on the Appalachian Trail, a tiny stream of water trickles from a two-inch iron pipe. This is Ice Water Spring. (Do not drink the water without boiling or purifying it.)

After the spring the trail descends a bit more steeply, sometimes over a stony pathway. Views to North Carolina continue on the right.

In about 3.5 miles the trail returns to the Smokies crest. Here, less than half a mile from the Bunion, the climax of the Walk begins. For here the crest is narrow. You are walking on top of a ridge that is sometimes only six feet wide. Through the stunted beeches, birches and spruces, you can see mountains on both sides of you. On your right is the long ridge of Richland Mountain, which runs south from the crest, and the lower, more distant summits of North Carolina rolling on to the southern horizon. On your left and close by are the steep slopes of Mount Kephart and the Jumpoff. Behind Kephart is LeConte. Between the two is the Boulevard. Ahead of you, less than a mile away, is 5,288-foot-high Horseshoe Mountain. To the right is the long ridge of Porters Mountain. Between Horseshoe and Porters mountains and plunging 1,000 feet down the clifflike slope in front of you is the deep, steepsided valley of Lester Prong. In the distance, beyond the boundary of the park, you can see the low hills of East Tennessee. Compared to the peaks in front of you

Cliff Top on **Mount LeConte** *(Walk No. 20) is famous for its sunsets.* ▶

they look almost flat.

Soon you can see the Bunion itself, rising steeply up the right-hand side of the green, forested valley in front of you like the remains of a very old and very ruined Bavarian castle. From the depths of the valley, long buttresses of rough gray ledge, one behind the other, sweep upward to rocky knobs like swags of cloth, then sweep up again to other knobs, then up again until they reach the stone ramparts of the Bunion, a natural gray rock edifice that, just like a well-situated medieval fortress, sits astride the narrow, steep crest more than 1,000 feet above almost everything beneath it.

As you walk toward the Bunion, you not only see but feel that you are now on top of a world of giddy steepness. The only thing that's level is the path you're walking on. And as you stroll along the narrow, mile-high crest — higher than almost everything you can see — and look at the circle of hills plunging down to the valley in front of you, you feel light.

Resist, however, the temptation to skip along to the Bunion. You are literally in the middle of the most dramatic mountain scenery in the Smokies. Walk as you would walk in an art gallery. Savor the views slowly, carefully. Make the beauty last.

All too quickly the trail splits. The right fork goes past the Bunion. The left fork is the best 300 feet of trail in the Smokies. It's the shelf that runs like a *corniche* all around the edge of the Bunion, providing continuous and incomparable vistas of the awesome terrain below.

As you start walking the *corniche* look across the cirquelike valley to your left. From left to right you see the Smokies crest, where you were only minutes ago; Mount Kephart and the steep slopes below the Jumpoff; the Boulevard, Mount LeConte and, in front of you, Horseshoe Mountain.

About 100 feet from the trail fork you'll come to an eight-foot-high, 14-foot-long knob perched on the point of the Bunion. From this point on the trail you'll have a 300-degree view: everything you just saw, as well as the long rock ramparts of the Bunion and the steep, spruce-and-fir-coated slopes of Porters Mountain that plunge at a 45-degree angle down to the valley of Porters Creek.

Continue walking around the Bunion and the view gets even better. You look downward into a great bowl and there is steepness everywhere: in the cliffs of the Bunion beneath your feet and in the slopes of Horse-shoe and Porters mountains opposite the Bunion, all of which plunge down, down, down to the forested valley 2,000 feet below. If you can take your eyes off the views, notice as well the thick, handsome patches of sand myrtle and little-leaf rhododendron growing on both sides of the path. A few feet of this trail are narrow, incidentally, and there are no cables or handholds anywhere on the Bunion. So watch your step.

The Bunion's views suddenly stop when the *corniche* rejoins the main trail. Only about .1 miles beyond this intersection, however, the Appalachian Trail runs through a grassy heath bald. From here you have a long view down the valley of Kephart Prong. Richland Mountain is to the left of the valley. Mount Kephart is to the right.

Turn around here and follow the Appalachian Trail back to Newfound Gap. Needless to say, take a right where the trail forks near the Bunion and, slowly, deliberately, enjoy the views from the *corniche* once again.

And contemplate how this magnificent natural edifice was so badly misnamed. According to local legend, one of the people who once hiked here was one Charlie Connor, who had long suffered from an unusually large bunion. When one of his companions looked at the rocky knob he supposedly said: "That sticks out like Charlie's bunion." Thus, ironically, was one of the most unsavory names in the Smokies applied to one of its most magnificent features. Thank God Shakespeare was right: As a rose by any other name would smell as sweet, so the splendor of Charlies Bunion rises magnificently above its moniker.

20 Mount LeConte

This two-day outing to the top of the third-highest peak in the Smokies is really four walks in one. On the first day you walk 7.7 miles to the summit of LeConte, traveling first on the Smokies crest, then on the Boulevard, a nearly level, mile-high ridge with all-but-continuous views on both sides. After dinner at LeConte Lodge you walk the .2-mile trail to Cliff Top, where you watch the sun set behind Sugarland Mountain. After spend-

---

Fog in the valleys looks like silver lakes just after sunrise at Myrtle Point on **Mount LeConte** *(Walk No. 20).* ▶

ing the night in a cozy log cabin, you get up before dawn (if you like) and walk the three-quarter-mile-long trail to Myrtle Point, where you can see the sun rise over the Smokies crest. After breakfast at the lodge you walk down the steep-sided mountain on the 5.5-mile-long Alum Cave Trail (Walk No. 18), where you enjoy frequent views of Mingus and Sugarland mountains, the deep valley of Walker Camp Prong and the West Prong of the Little Pigeon River and the many shoulders of LeConte.

Unfortunately, cabins at the lodge may be the most popular accommodations in the Smokies. Most people who stay in them make their reservations almost a year in advance. On any given day, *every* cabin will have been reserved for months. As we noted in the introduction, however, cancellations do occur. So if you arrive in the Smokies without a reservation, we suggest you call the lodge every day, at 615-429-5704, until they get a cancellation.

If you can't get a reservation before you have to leave the Smokies, you have several other choices. You could walk up and down the mountain in one day, but that's a wearisome excursion and you'd miss both the sunset and the sunrise. You could also camp out at the Le-Conte Shelter but you'd have to carry a heavy pack, sleep on a wooden platform and so forth. Or you could make a reservation for next year. The decision, of course, is yours but only the third choice would make LeConte a Great Walk.

You also have a choice of five different trails that go

to the top of LeConte. Three of them—the Bullhead, Rainbow Falls and Trillium Gap—are long, hard climbs with only occasional views. Another one, Alum Cave, is steep in places but it's only 5.5 miles long and highly scenic (see Walk No. 18). The fifth trail—actually a combination of the Appalachian and Boulevard Trails—is 7.7 miles long but it's often level, never steep and, like the Alum Cave Trail, loaded with views. Not surprisingly, most people agree that *one* of the last two trails is the best way to climb LeConte. Many people argue that Alum Cave is the best trail because its (relative) brevity and outstanding views outweigh its steepness, whereas the Boulevard approach is simply too long. Others prefer the Boulevard because its gentleness and its own uncommon views make its length easy to bear. They also say there's a better chance of seeing wildlife on the Boulevard Trail than on the more heavily traveled Alum Cave Trail. (Which is probably true. The last time we were on the Boulevard Trail a fawn actually walked to within 12 feet of us. On the other hand, we've never seen a deer or any other large animal on the Alum Cave Trail.) Actually it doesn't matter which trail is best because *both* trails are worth walking and, happily, a trip up and down LeConte lets you do exactly that. We suggest, however, that you go up LeConte on the Boulevard Trail and save the steeper Alum Cave Trail for your descent.

Like the Walk to Charlies Bunion (No. 19), the ascent of LeConte via the Boulevard Trail begins in Newfound Gap and follows the Appalachian Trail to the Boulevard Trail junction. If you're lucky enough to have two cars at your disposal, leave one at the Newfound Gap parking area and the other at the Alum

Cave Trail parking lot. If you have only one car leave it at Newfound Gap. When you get to the Alum Cave Trail parking lot at the end of your trip, find someone who's heading for Newfound Gap — it's only five miles away — and ask him or her for a ride.

After walking the Appalachian Trail for 2.7 miles, go left on the Boulevard Trail and immediately start a gentle climb. In just a few hundred feet you'll pass the trail to the Jumpoff on your right. Immediately after the intersection the Boulevard Trail starts a gradual descent of the north slope of Mount Kephart. The mountainside drops steeply on your left and rises sharply on your right. On your left, through giant spruces and firs, you can see the Smokies' crest running from Newfound Gap to Clingmans Dome. Your destination, Mount LeConte, rises ahead of you.

The last time we were here — a cold, mid-October day — we were shrouded in white fog; we could see only a few dozen feet ahead of us. But the branches of the evergreens had an elegant white, snowlike coat of hoarfrost and the moss on both sides of the trail was thick and rich. We had no views but, even though winter was two months away, we were in a white-and-green winter wonderland.

After crossing the tiny and sometimes dry headwaters of Walker Camp Prong the trail levels off. Then,

View from the Alum Cave Trail just below Cliff Top on **Mount LeConte** *(Walk No. 20). In the foreground: the red berries of mountain ash. In the distance: the slopes of Sugarland Mountain and the receding blue ridges that look like the waves of a choppy sea.*
◀

about 3.6 miles from Newfound Gap, you come to a clearing and an overlook on the right. There's a five-foot-long log bench here and, ten feet away from it, a large fir tree that has fallen over the edge of the steep slope. Its flat roots are upended; they're now a huge wheel of tangled, crooked spokes rising 12 feet off the ground. Beyond the dead fir you can see the deep valley of Shutts Prong and, further on, the valley of the Little Pigeon River. Horseshoe Mountain is just ahead of you. Porters Mountain is beyond it. Greenbrier Pinnacle is in the distance (a band of ledge known as the Catstairs runs across its western slope). Farthest away, outside the park, is the mesalike hump of English Mountain and the Great Valley of the Tennessee River.

You'll see slightly different versions of this view for the next three miles as the trail runs on or very near the almost level crest of the Boulevard. You'll also glimpse different versions of the view to the left of the ridge: Mount LeConte, at the end of the Boulevard, and Anakeesta Ridge, which runs west from the Boulevard toward the valley of Walker Camp Prong. You'll also see where you just came from: Newfound Gap, the Newfound Gap Road and, behind you, the Smokies' crest and Mount Kephart.

This long gallery of views is clearest after late October, when the beeches, birches and other hardwoods have lost their leaves and only spruces and firs (many of the latter denuded by balsam woolly adelgids) stand between you and the vistas.

About five miles from Newfound Gap the trail climbs gently to the crest of the eastern end of Anakeesta Ridge and, in front of a large dying fir tree, switches back sharply to the right and descends to Alum Gap. Here, on your left, you can see into the valley of Alum Cave Creek and, beyond the valley, Peregrine Ridge and the landslide-scarred slopes of LeConte.

From here the trail continues its easy progress along the Boulevard. Sometimes the trail is level, sometimes it gently climbs and sometimes it gradually descends. One minute it follows the very top of the crest. The next minute it runs just to the left of it, then just to the right. Sometimes you see only rhododendrons and trees. At other times you have views — one moment on your left, another on your right and sometimes on both sides of the long, narrow ridge at once. You not only see but *feel* that you're on top of a linear platform in the sky.

As you get closer to LeConte, you see more things on your left: heath balds on the slopes of Mount LeConte; Sugarland Mountain rising up on the west side of the valley of the West Prong of the Little Pigeon River; Clingmans Dome, the highest place in the park, five miles southwest of Newfound Gap; fir-topped Anakeesta Knob on Anakeesta Ridge, now behind you, and, of all things (and just briefly) the parking lot back at Newfound Gap.

Also to your rear, but on the right side of the Boulevard, you start to see the ridge on which you just walked and, to the left of the Boulevard, landmarks of the Smokies' crest: Mount Kephart, the Jumpoff, Charlies Bunion, the jagged Sawteeth and other points to the northeast.

Finally, almost six miles from Newfound Gap, the trail switches sharply back to the left. Here, in an opening on the right side of the ridge, you have 180-degree views. You can see all the way from the Great Valley of the Tennessee River on your left to the major peaks of the Smokies' crest on your right.

Beyond this point the trail starts climbing the precipitous northeastern slopes of LeConte. The cliffs of Myrtle Point rise steeply on the left. The walls of ravines — headwaters of the Boulevard Prong and Lowes and Cannon creeks — drop even more steeply on your right. Your views are now only to your right but they are all but uninterrupted — especially in the late fall — and they range from English Mountain and the sinuous curve of Lake Douglas ahead of you to the Smokies' crest and Mount Kephart to your far right. The trail is now the essence of a Great Walk: a linear observation platform with almost continuous views of spectacular mountain scenery.

The trail becomes even more exposed as it follows the rocky shelf up the steep mountain. Sand myrtle and little-leaf rhododendrons — denizens of cold, windy, rocky places — appear on both sides of the trail. As you pass rock slides and peer into the ravines on your right you think: It's a long way down. The trail, however, is neither difficult nor dangerous, just exciting.

In less than a mile the path enters a spruce-and-fir forest (leaving the views temporarily behind), switches back to the left and, almost 7.5 miles from Newfound Gap, passes the trail to Myrtle Point on the left. Tomorrow morning you can take this trail to watch the sun rise.

A few hundred feet past the Myrtle Point Trail the Boulevard Trail levels off. Here, about 20 feet to the left of the trail, is a 12-foot-wide, six-foot-high rock cairn that marks the location of High Top, the highest point on LeConte.

Then the trail starts descending and quickly comes to

a tiny clearing at the edge of a steep slope that's thick with little-leaf rhododendrons. From this vantage point you can see almost every place you just walked. In front of you is what looks like one long, unbroken ridge, a giant S-curve that winds from Newfound Gap, three miles away, and takes in the Smokies' crest, the Boulevard and landslide-scarred Myrtle Point.

The trail reenters the woods but through the trees on the left you can see the valley of Walker Camp Prong, Newfound Gap, Clingmans Dome and, beyond the Smokies' crest, wave after wave of mountain ridges in North Carolina.

The trail quickly passes the fieldstone Mount LeConte Shelter on the left and, immediately after the shelter, reaches a large grassy clearing, also on the left, where angelica grows profusely. Here you have a much clearer view toward Newfound Gap. (Here, too, a .3-mile-long side trail leads to Cliff Tops, where you can watch the sun set tonight.)

In just a couple of hundred feet you come to a trail junction where the Trillium Gap Trail goes right, the Rainbow Falls Trail goes straight ahead and the Boulevard Trail ends. Here, on your right, you also see for the first time the rustic log buildings of LeConte Lodge — a welcome sight after a nearly eight-mile walk.

Follow the Rainbow Falls Trail for about 100 feet. On your left you'll see the beginning of another, shorter (.2-mile) trail to Cliff Top. On your right you'll see the entrance path to the lodge, the highest resort east of the Rocky Mountains. And one of the most uncommon.

Accommodations here are primitive but comfortable. You sleep, for example, in one of ten private "guest cabins" furnished with charming, Adirondack-style log beds with mattresses and box springs and made up with sheets and blankets—just like in a hotel. Unlike a hotel, however, the cabins have no electricity, central heat, running water or plumbing. Like every other building at the lodge, they're lit by kerosene lamps and warmed by kerosene heaters. You wash in a metal basin with water you draw from a nearby central spigot and heat in a large kettle on the kerosene heater. You also provide your own washcloth and towel. And the toilets are in another building. Even though we had to live a bit like the pioneer farmers who built the log cabins seen throughout the park (see Walks No. 14-16), it didn't bother us at all. The heaters kept the cabin warm even on cold fall nights (even with a window open for ventilation) and they quickly heated up more than enough water for us to get as clean as we could have gotten in a shower. The kerosene lamps (with help from our flashlights) gave us all the light we needed. We were as comfortable here as we would have been in a motel. In fact, our nights spent on top of this mountain, in a warm, snug cabin lit by the candlelike flicker of an oil lamp, were our best nights in the Smokies.

Like the cabins, meals at the lodge are basic but very satisfying. They're served family style (you can eat all you like) at six long tables in a large wood-paneled dining room whose casement windows have views of the foothills of East Tennessee. Nearly all the food you eat for dinner at the lodge has been flown in by helicopter (along with the kerosene and most of the lodge's other supplies) at the beginning of the season. That means fruits, vegetables and meats are canned and salads are nonexistent. On the other hand, breads and cookies are homemade from staples on the premises.

Whether fresh or canned, however, everything we've eaten at the lodge has been tasty — and that's only partly because mountain air and exercise do wonders for the appetite.

Dinner almost always includes soup, homemade bread, meat, corn or potatoes, a vegetable, fruit and homemade cookies. The last night we were here, for example, we had homemade minestrone soup, hot homemade cornbread, corn, turnip greens (popular in the South) and a delicious ham. Dessert was peaches and homemade cookies. Wine is also available for an extra charge.

Breakfast is usually scrambled eggs (fresh), ham or bacon, grits (another Southern dish, made from corn), pancakes and Tang.

Coffee, tea and hot chocolate are served with all meals and are also available in the dining room all day at no extra charge.

All this — a private cabin and two ample meals — costs less than a motel room and two comparable meals in Gatlinburg. And if you spend two or more nights here, the lodge also provides a substantial box lunch on your second day on the mountain. The last time we were here we had a choice of corned beef or cheese on large, thick slices of homemade bread; a box of raisins, a bag of trail mix (nuts, raisins and sunflower seeds) and a homemade chocolate cookie.

The lodge, a regulated Park Service concession, has no plans to expand its present capacity of just 50 people, the number that can fit in the dining room. General Manager Tim Line says a bigger crowd would "spoil the experience."

It's a legitimate worry. For LeConte is more than the

sum of its accommodations. Staying here *is* an "experience," one of the best in the Smokies. Before we came here we didn't know if we'd enjoy having dinner with a table full of strangers. We needn't have worried. On the contrary, the ice was broken instantly and warm and lively conversation quickly turned strangers into friends. Maybe it's something about this place. Or the mountain. Or the people who come here. Or some combination of all three.

Actually, more than half the people who stay here have stayed here before, some of them many times. Many people come back every year. It's not hard to see why.

After dinner, get a flashlight and climb the .2-mile-long trail to Cliff Top, which begins opposite the lodge. Cliff Top is best known as the place to watch the sun set. But it has at least two other things to recommend it.

One is simply the view. From its jagged ledge, 6,500 feet in the air, you have a 180-degree view up and down the valley of Walker Camp Prong and the West Prong of the Little Pigeon River, half a mile below you. From left to right the mountain panorama includes Newfound Gap; the Smokies' crest and its highest point, Clingmans Dome; the long ridges of Mingus and Sugarland mountains and the twin rock peaks of the Chimney Tops on a spur of Sugarland, almost 2,000 feet below you. Beyond Sugarland Mountain, blue ridge after blue ridge extends to the horizon. Farther to the right, you can see the outskirts of Gatlinburg and the foothills of East Tennessee. On your far right are West and Balsam points, both shoulders or spurs of LeConte.

Cliff Top's other notable feature is its natural landscaping. Here, at the very edge of a mountaintop, nature has created an exquisite rock garden consisting of just two things: jagged ledge and large, neat drifts of little-leaf rhododendron growing vigorously all around you and down the cliffs in front of you. Cliff Top is one of those rare and precious natural things: a bit of nature so tidily perfect that there is nothing a landscape gardener could do to make it better.

Then, of course, there's the sunset, which on a clear fall day turns the mountains indigo and the sky orange and then pink. As the sky darkens, you can see the lights of Knoxville twinkling 50 miles away.

When you're ready to return, turn on your flashlight and retrace your steps to the lodge.

It's natural to go to bed early on LeConte, partly because you're tired and partly because there's no TV or other electronic distraction to keep you up. That's good, because it makes it easier for you to get up early enough to walk to Myrtle Point to watch the sun rise. (The lodge crew will lend you an alarm clock if you need one.)

To get the most out of this Walk don't try to sleep to the last possible moment and then dash out to the point. Allow yourself enough time to retrace your steps along the Boulevard Trail to where the quarter-mile trail to Myrtle Point begins about half a mile from the lodge. That way you won't be rushed. You'll be able to savor the softness of the predawn woods (and perhaps see a deer) and to enjoy the often mystical beauty of the view from the point that occurs *before* the sun rises. (Be sure to bring along a flashlight in case the predawn light is still too dark for you to make out the path.)

The trail to Myrtle Point curves through the forest at

or near the top of a long and increasingly narrow ridge. The path ends at the wide, rolling ledge (or "point") where the ridge abruptly stops and plunges into the valleys below. The ledge is thickly grown with little-leaf rhododendron and (appropriately) sand myrtle, and the view from here is nearly panoramic. On your left you can see around the north side of Mount LeConte to Pigeon Forge, Tennessee. On your right you can see Sugarland Mountain and the valley of the West Prong of the Little Pigeon River. In between, along the long arc of the horizon, are most of the major peaks of the Smokies.

If you're lucky you will have arrived here at least 15 minutes before sunrise. At that time you won't see the distant mountains clearly. Instead you may see ice-blue fog—some of the Smokies' famous smoke—filling the bottoms of the valleys and the tops of indigo mountains rising like islands from the lakes of fog. You'll see ridge after ridge of deep blue mountains rippling to the horizon all around you, their crests etched as crisply and delicately as a Japanese ink wash against the banks of fog behind them. Straight ahead of you the eastern sky is amber. Just before dawn, on some days, it will be rose colored.

When sunrise finally begins over the Smokies' crest the horizon, ironically, will be too bright to identify the mountains closest to the sun. Block out the sun with your hand for a moment and, in October at least, you'll see the Jumpoff and the steep sides of Mount Kephart to the right of the sun and the even steeper ledges of Charlies Bunion to the left. You'll also see what looks like the outline of every tree on top of the Smokies' crest.

The daytime view from Myrtle Point isn't as exciting as that from other places on LeConte. Too many mountains are simply too far away. That's why the best time to be here is before and during sunrise, not after. So when the rosy light of dawn turns white, go back to the lodge and enjoy a hearty breakfast.

When you're ready to climb down the mountain, get back on the Rainbow Falls Trail (go right as you leave the lodge) and follow it less than .1 miles to a fork. The Rainbow Falls Trail goes right here; the Alum Cave Trail goes left.

Follow the Alum Cave Trail through a tunnel of spruce trees, after which the nearly level (but here slightly stony) trail curves around the north side of Mount LeConte. On your right, through the defoliated branches of dead and dying fir trees, you can see Gatlinburg and Pigeon Forge almost a mile below.

The trail keeps curving around to the west side of the mountain and passes under the precipitous slopes of Cliff Top.

Suddenly you come to the most exciting place on Mount LeConte. The trail is now a shelf in the steep rocky face of the mountain, like the *corniche* at Charlies Bunion. The slope rises almost straight up on your left and drops sharply down on your right. You feel that you are literally on the edge of the mountain. There are steel cables on your left so you can have something to hold on to if the trail is slippery or icy. Ahead of you is more steepness: the slope of LeConte plunges down to the valley of the West Prong of the Little Pigeon River and, to the right of the deep V of the valley, the slopes of Sugarland Mountain spring steeply up. In the distance the tops of exquisite blue ridges rise like the waves of a choppy sea. As at Charlies Bunion, there's steepness all around you.

The views continue as you walk easily along the cliffy slope of LeConte. Rock outcrops rise dramatically above you. Dense clumps of little-leaf rhododendron and sand myrtle turn the trail into a cliff garden. Ahead of you are evergreen-coated ridges and Newfound Gap. On your right, hundreds of feet below, is the valley of Trout Branch, which runs off Mount LeConte. Below, and perpendicular to Trout Branch, is the long valley of the West Prong. On the other side of the valley is the long ridge of Sugarland Mountain.

The trail soon passes over the scars of a landslide. Dead trees, uprooted by the slide, lie in a jumble down the slope.

Shortly thereafter the trail crosses a sunny, grassy bald and, later, the remains of another landslide and its huge tangled detritus of trees.

About a mile from the lodge the trail climbs down 23 log steps and switches back to the right. Now the trail heads out on the long ridge that rises between the valley of Trout Branch, which is on your right, and the valley of Styx Branch and Alum Cave Creek, which is at the bottom of the steep slope on your left. Rising 2,000 feet above the valley to your left are the equally steep slopes of Anakeesta Ridge. There's more moisture in the ground here than in the thin, ledgy soil you were just walking on. So you're now in the shade of large spruces, firs and hemlocks, and rhododendron, laurel and leucothoe grow on both sides of the trail.

The path soon levels out and gradually crosses to the north side of the ridge. To your right you can see where you were only a few minutes ago: the grassy bald, the landslide scars and the cliffs on the steep western face of LeConte.

Then the trail curves to the left around a high, almost vertical ledge. Steel cables are attached to the rock in case you need to hold on to them. As you round the ledge you see Sugarland Mountain to your right. Then you see Peregrine Ridge, perpendicular to the trail, on your right, and another view of Anakeesta Ridge ahead of you.

Soon you're at the enormous, tan Alum Cave Bluffs. Take a look at the "cave," then continue following the trail 2.5 miles to its trailhead on the Newfound Gap Road. If you've already taken the Alum Cave Trail (Walk No. 18) from the Newfound Gap Road to the cave, the route will be familiar to you. If you haven't taken that Walk, refer to our description of it and follow its directions from the trailhead to the cave in reverse.

Great Smokies Poster Available

A larger version of the picture of the sunset on Mount LeConte on page 97 has been made into a dazzling poster titled *The Great Smokies*. Copies are available for $9.95 each, plus $3 for handling and shipping in a protective tube, from Great Walks, PO Box 410, Goffstown, NH 03045.